Towards a POLITICAL THEOLOGY

Significance of a Multigenerational Memoir

OTIS CLAYTON, SR.

ⒾiUniverse

TOWARDS A POLITICAL THEOLOGY
SIGNIFICANCE OF A MULTIGENERATIONAL MEMOIR

Scripture quotations marked NKJV are taken from the New King James Version. Copyright © 1982 by Thomas Nelson, Inc. Used by permission. All rights reserved.

iUniverse books may be ordered through booksellers or by contacting:

iUniverse
1663 Liberty Drive
Bloomington, IN 47403
www.iuniverse.com
844-349-9409

ISBN: 978-1-6632-5157-2 (sc)
ISBN: 978-1-6632-5158-9 (e)

Library of Congress Control Number: 2023907104

Print information available on the last page.

iUniverse rev. date: 01/09/2024

I dedicate this book to the legacy and memory of my parents, Aaron (Otis) Clayton and Elizabeth Murphy-Clayton, siblings, grandparents, other relatives, dear friends, and our ancestors.

CONTENTS

PREFACE

I am a Christian Clergyman and a Baptist Preacher. I have served in ministry for over fifty years. In this capacity, I have served as a pastor and United States Army Chaplain. I obtained preparation for the church by studying at several colleges, seminaries, and universities, one of which is the Vanderbilt University School of Divinity. This book is about my ministry journey towards developing my understanding of political theology. To this extent, I think about my own religious and spiritual upbringing as an African American from my childhood experience up to the present time. I have learned from my ancestors and political theologians like Martin Luther King, Jr. Indeed, my ancestors may have been uneducated. Still, they fought against slavery and oppression in their community, and through lessons learned, they passed their thinking about religion and how it could be used as a tool towards liberation and freedom. Theologians who led social movements to liberate oppressed and marginalized people have helped me think about political theology more rationally and theoretically. Therefore, my goal now is to pass on my development of political theology to family members and friends.

I wrote this book after I spent some time as a member of The Porch. This community for writers in metropolitan Nashville, Tennessee, was co-founded by Susannah Felts and Katie McDougall. As a member of Porch, I was encouraged to take my intellectual understanding of political theology and make it more personal. Before becoming a Porch member, I pursued post-doctoral studies at Canterbury Christ Church University in Canterbury, England (The United Kingdom). So, I took my post-doctoral research project and turned it into something more personal. I wrote this book sitting at home in Hendersonville, Tennessee. This book includes a trajectory of my childhood years and letters that I wrote to family members, friends, and former university professors. Of course, I wrote this book primarily to describe how I have come to understand the subject of political theology from the past to the present.

INTRODUCTION

In Spring 2017, I began post-doctoral studies in Religion at Canterbury Christ Church University (CCCU) in Canterbury, England (Great Britain). Professor Robert Beckford was my major in the Department of Humanities in the Spring of 2017. At that time, I developed a particular interest in political theology. Professor Beckford authored Dread and Pentecostal: A Political Theology for the Black Church in Britain, for which I developed a particular appetite. Subsequently, I wanted to write a thesis about my specific understanding of political theology. I was interested in researching and writing about political theology for the Black Lives Matter movement. Simultaneously, at that time, I began to become sadly and interestingly annoyed by a former military lower back injury, so much so that I took a medical leave from CCCU. I returned home to America to have a surgical procedure, which required rehabilitation and physical therapy.

Additionally, to my amazement, I discovered that my beloved Mother, Elizabeth Murphy-Clayton, illness and sickness were becoming increasingly more challenging and more problematic. So, after consulting with my siblings and my friend and mentor, Professor Lewis V. Baldwin, I decided to withdraw from CCCU and turn my attention primarily toward teaching, preaching, and writing.

Shortly after that, I relocated from Aurora, Colorado, to metropolitan Nashville Davidson County to live closer to my mother and help my sibling as we provided care for Mother Elizabeth. Living in the community, I consequently became a member of the Porch, a friendly and loving community for writers in Nashville. I made a class presentation in a personal writing class taught by Susan Felts. She and Katie McDougall are Co-Founders of the Porch. Susan suggested that I take my project and make it more personal. Subsequently, the rest is now history. Towards a Political Theology: A Multigenerational Memoir attempts to make my view of political theology more personal and approachable.

On December 7, 2022, at approximately 10:57 PM, I stood at my Mother's bedside, Elizabeth, in Memphis, Tennessee, with my youngest brother, La Shun. Our loving mother went home to live with God and our ancestors. My book here is dedicated to the life and legacy of my parents, Aaron and Elizabeth Clayton, our ancestors, African diaspora people, humanity, and the environment.

The following is a basic outline of this book to make my political theology personal and approachable to the general public. The first chapter describes my formative early childhood years during the civil rights movement of the 1950s, and my thinking continues to develop up to the present. My fraternal grandfather and other ancestors insisted that, although we lived in a segregated society, we needed to pursue a quality education at all costs. This mindset is reflected in succeeding chapters.

Chapters two through eight (8) are epistolary letters. These were letters written to family members, friends, and mentors to explain my thinking about history, theology, and philosophy. My son, grandson, niece, brother, and friend's letters reflect on some personal struggles and tragedies we have endured to survive and prosper in America and the universe.

The letter to my grandson gave him a family and historical understanding of the Christian ministry and religion. Hopefully, my letter will provide him with an appreciation of history as it enables him to look forward to achieving his goals and objectives.

The letter to my son is an effort to awaken and shake him up from any naivete understanding that he may have about his family history and heritage. In the process, he will become more aware of family history, which challenges him to become more politically engaged.

The letter to my niece Tanya is one of love and support. Like some of us, she embraces LGBTQ sensitivity. This is certainly an attitude and mentality of living within a diverse and progressive society. So, with that in mind, I want to let her know that I love and appreciate her completely.

The letter to my younger brother, Terry, the attorney, is a letter that could be addressed to all of our family members. This is a letter that is both retrospective and prospective. This letter to Terry reminds us how far God has us as a family and a people and how far we must go. We know that we are indeed in need of American Criminal Justice Reform.

The letter to my friend Reverend Edward Thompson allows me to present a reflection on our initial meeting, our friendship, and how Reverend Thompson's skills and abilities were significant in helping me to understand better community organizing. Reverend Thompson, at the time of the writing of this book, is the President of the Nashville Organization for Hope and Action (NOHA). It is a community organization in Nashville Davidson County.

My letters to Professor Lewis Baldwin and Professor Robert Beckford are pivotal. Although these letters are personal and professional, my letter to Baldwin and Beckford reflects on scholarly expertise regarding political theology related to ministry, social activism, and, most importantly, climate justice reform. Further, my letter to Beckford reveals something kind of paradoxical. Beckford view about the Black Pentecostal Church in Great Britain is equally appropriate for Black Americans, particularly as it relates to the idea of reparations for persons of the African diaspora. Indeed, I have made the letter to Professor Beckford my first letter.

Indeed, these letters reveal some of my thinking and development as a clergy member in the African-American religious experience. Historically, the clergy has always been actively involved with social and political challenges and opportunities to make America a more just and equal society for everyone. Meanwhile, my letters here serve as a watershed event to educate his sibling and others that the struggle for African Americans' human dignity continues. Essentially, my letters present and suggest actions needed to develop political theology. Hopefully, the reader is left with this question to ponder: What is my political theology toward progressive change in America?

Chapter 1

MY LETTER TO DR. ROBERT BECKFORD ON POLITICAL THEOLOGY (REPARATIONS)

Frederick Ware: An Introduction to Black Theology

I was excited to r6eceive my letter of acceptance to become a post-doctoral student at the Canterbury Christ Church University in Canterbury, England. I entered this phase of my education with a diverse background and training in theology and philosophy. I earned a master of divinity degree with a concentration in theology, a master of arts degree in philosophy, and a doctoral degree in homiletics with a concentration in theology. Also, I taught courses in theology at the Tennessee School of Religion and served many years as pastor and United States Army chaplain. So, in this respect, I knew I could complete the CCCU program.

Frederick (Fred) Ware is a mutual friend of ours. He has served with you as a member of the International Pentecostal Council and in other religious capacities. Fred and I met in the mid-1980s when we studied philosophy at Memphis State University (now called the University of Memphis). I came to the university to study philosophy right after I completed my studies at the Memphis Theological Seminary. As Fred and I studied philosophy, we became fast friends. At the time, no more than three African Americans were in the department. Also, Fred and I were ministers in different faith traditions. While he was a minister in the Church of God in Christ (Pentecostal) tradition, I was a minister with Central Baptist Church Incorporated. Although we were ministers within different faith traditions, we shared the same cultural heritage as members of the African-American religious experience.

Sometimes, before and after class, we discussed philosophy and religion from antiquity to the present. After all, we were essentially African-American Christians studying philosophy. Cornel West and James Cones were African-American academicians we could quickly identify with. They were examples of what we could become. They were scholars who taught their various disciplines at Union Theological Seminary. West was taught courses in philosophy. *Prophesy Deliverance! An Afro-American Revolutionary Christianity* (1982) by West was one of the many texts we discussed. He demonstrated that there was no disconnect between philosophy and the way believers practice their faith. He told anyone he encountered about his religious and cultural heritage. He was a Christian who was the grandson of a Black Baptist clergy member and was a devoted follower of the radical faith of Jesus Christ.

Likewise, we discussed *A Black Theology of Liberation* (1970) by James Cone. Like West, Cone's book also reflected a radical understanding of Christianity with more of a biblical framework because he used the Bible, particularly the synoptic gospels, to support his theological claims.

In Fred's second book, *African American Theology: An Introduction* (2016), he demonstrates his comprehensive philosophical and theological training and our long friendship. He wrote:

> My experience as a student and now teacher parallels shifting perceptions of African-American theology in the last thirty-two years. In the spring semester of 1984, while I was an undergraduate student in philosophy at Memphis State University (now the University of Memphis), I was introduced to Black theology by Otis Clayton. Otis, a recent seminary graduate, was enrolled in the master's program in philosophy. We talked often and at length before and after our course in the philosophy of religion. Otis's command of the literature and coherent summaries of the debates in Black theology convinced me that Black theology was a field of study that I needed to know … While preparing this book, as fate would have it, I had the privilege, after nearly ten years since our last conversation, to speak again with Otis. By his present question and tone, I sense his unease with recent works in Black theology, especially those that purport to do theology without

> a professed commitment to fundamental
> Christian beliefs. (p.xi).

I completed my degree in philosophy one year before Fred and went on to study theology and philosophy briefly at Boston University. It was primarily because of the legacy and life of Martin Luther King Jr. that I decided to attend that particular university. Although he completed his PhD in systematic theology, King went to the study at the university because he wanted to study personalistic philosophy, which proposes that the clue to the meaning of ultimate reality is found in personality. (M.L. King Jr. *Stride Toward Freedom: The Montgomery Story (1958)*, p.100) It is also sometimes called Boston personalism, which was promulgated by Edgar S. Brightman.

Brightman died shortly after King began his studies, and then Harold De Wolf, one of Brightman's former students, became King's principal advisor. De Wolf guided King through the completion of his degree. During my studies at Boston University, I took several classes and courses from professors who had mentored, or taught Martin Luther King Jr. Professor Walter Muelder was one of his mentors and former close associates. Muelder, Harold De Wolf, and others from Boston University met privately with King and provided him counsel throughout his leadership and involvement in the civil rights movement. So, like Muelder and De Wolf, King was an adherent of the philosophy of Boston personalism.

When I arrived to pursue my post-graduate studies at Boston University, I realized that a metamorphosis had occurred since King studied there. A Ph.D. in systematic theology was no longer offered; it had been replaced by a Ph.D. in ethics. However, I had the opportunity to pursue a PhD in theology through the Boston School of Theology.

Admittedly, while studying there, I had a cathartic kind of experience. I enjoyed the cultural and academic environment of Boston. Of course, I mixed and mingled with a cross-section of persons of different races and religions, which reminded me of my military experiences and the time I spent studying philosophy at the University of Memphis. Also, there were various higher learning institutions in Boston, such as Boston College and Harvard University. I enjoyed a high level of intellectual stimulation in this unique and splendid educational environment.

Additionally, at that time, I could take a personal inventory of my financial situation. I was relatively impoverished, and I compared my financial situation to that of most of my fellow students. Unlike my fellow students, I was able to study at Boston University because of financial aid, and I obtained a student loan. However, I saw undergraduate and graduate students who did not experience the financial difficulties that I was experiencing. I saw fellow students wearing the best clothes and expensive jewelry. Any number of them drove BMW, Mercedes-Benz, and Cadillac automobiles.

King's financial situation was vastly different from my own. When he came to study at Boston University, he earned a fellowship from Crozer Theological Seminary to pursue his post-graduate education. In addition, his father was the pastor of the financially powerful and influential Ebenezer Baptist Church in Atlanta, Georgia.

To demonstrate the financial support, he received from his family, King's parents purchased him a new car to drive around Boston or anywhere else. So, after thinking about my financial considerations, I talked with my family and pastor and decided that I needed to withdraw from the university and return to my home in Memphis to reassess my dream and decide on the best way to earn a doctoral degree.

Several years after I returned from Boston University, Fred and I reconnected. We met at the Vanderbilt University Divinity School library, and I invited him to preach to my new congregation at the Mount Zion Freewill Baptist Church in Goodwin, Arkansas. That Sunday morning, Fred preached a powerful, moving, thought-provoking sermon. After his sermon, I invited him to talk with me in my church office. As we spoke, he took a copy of his book, *Methodologies in Black Theology* (2008), from his briefcase. He autographed his book and gave it to me. He wrote, "To my friend and brother, The Reverend Dr. Otis Clayton Sr. He was the first person to introduce me to the study of Black theology."

Advocate for the PhD program: Results in Gabriel _____, PhD

When I returned to Memphis after studying at Boston University, I attended courses in philosophy at the University of Memphis. During this time, I reacquainted myself with the faculty and staff of the department. Professors Hoke Robertson, Terry Hogan, Gene James, and Nancy Simco still taught their various classes. Hoke taught classes primarily on Emmanuel Kant and continental philosophy. Terry taught courses in the philosophy of science and epistemology. Although Gene and Nancy taught other classes from time to time—the history of philosophy, the philosophy of religion, and feminism—they also co-authored a classic textbook called *Elementary Logic* (1976).

I began to spend time with the faculty and attend philosophical conferences. I became incredibly close friends with a new faculty member, Professor Robert Bernasconi. He is a tall Englishman (roughly six foot four) and weighs about 230 pounds. Robert completed his doctorate in philosophy at the University of Essex. At our meeting, he held the chair of excellence in philosophy. But he teaches now at Penn State University and has written many articles and books in philosophy. *How to Read Sartre* (2006) is one of Robert's most recent books.

Robert and I talked endlessly about all areas of philosophy as well as the influence that the culture and history of Africa had on early Greek philosophy as they relate to the pre-Socratic and other philosophies. Although we had points of some disagreement, we discussed books written by African-American philosophers about that influence. These books included *Stolen Legacy: The Egyptian Origins of Western Philosophy* (1954) by George James and *Destruction of Black Civilizations: Great Issues of a Race from 4500 B.C. to 2000 A.D.* (1971) by Chancellor Williams.

Because of our friendship and mutual interest in philosophy and culture, I invited him to my mother's home for dinner, fellowship, and hospitality. Robert and I also enjoyed eating at soul food restaurants and touring historic

Beal Street to see and hear entertainers singing rhythm and blues. Linda Rogers, an entertainer on Beal Street, became one of Robert's favorite singers. Subsequently, he told me, "Otis, she invited me to attend her church, and I accepted her invitation and followed her to the New Bethel Full Gospel Baptist Church. It is an African American congregation." Although he was raised as a Roman Catholic, Robert worshipped and took an active part as a member and usher of that church. Like the other members, Robert enjoyed the music, joy, frenzy, and fellowship of that welcoming congregational environment.

I often referred to Robert as my brother by another mother. He was my blue-eyed soul brother. I believed that Robert used our friendship and relationship to recruit Black students and people of color into the Department of Philosophy. His interest to recruit such students to pursue careers in philosophy is unparalleled.

I had worked closely with him and other staff to develop a PhD in philosophy, and I was asked to make an application. I refused the offer, however, because of my desire to complete a PhD in systematic theology. Of course, I am delighted that my dear friend Robert Bernasconi did not allow my decision to deter him. He continued to pursue and aggressively recruit African American students and people of color to pursue a PhD at the University of Memphis.

Gabrielle _____, our mutual friend, is one student that Robert recruited. They met on one of his recruiting trips to Maryland. Gabrielle and Robert had much to talk about and discuss. After all, they were both citizens of Great Britain, but they had met in America. Also, she graduated from Morgan State University; the rest is history. She later earned a PhD in philosophy from the University of Memphis. And, because of my friendship and relationship with Robert Bernasconi and the University of Memphis Department of Philosophy, I am truly honored to know that I played a small part in helping that Ph.D. program to develop and strive through the participation of African Americans and people of color like Gabrielle Beckley-Raymond.

An Infatuation with Alistair Kee

Before I arrived at Canterbury Christ Church University (CCCU) campus, I did my due diligence to learn as much as possible about you and the faculty members with whom I must interface to graduate eventually. So, I talked with Frederick Ware, whom you know. He suggested that I speak directly with Eric Williams, whom Frederick Ware advised me was one of your former students.

You mentored Eric as he completed his doctorate at the University of Edinburgh. Eric continues to move forward with his career. As you may know, he is now a curator of religion at the Smithsonian Museum in Washington, DC. Eric told me that, in his estimation, you were like the James Cone of Great Britain. That spoke volumes to me about the kind of scholar you are. Like me, you were on the continuum more left of center. In short, you are incredibly progressive and prophetic in your theology.

We finally met at your CCCU campus office. At that meeting, although I had known about her, you introduced me to Gabrielle _____. You told me that I needed to learn four important things: (1) Gabrielle and you were two of three members who made up my doctoral committee;

(2) Gabrielle would be my first supervisor and first reader of my thesis topic and dissertation; (3) I needed to come up with a thesis proposal topic; and (4) I must read immediately Alistair Kee's book, *The Rise and Demise of Black Theology* (2008).

After our meeting concluded, I rushed to get Kee's book and get your book, *Dread and Pentecostal: A Political Theology for the Black Church in Britain* (2011). These books would broaden my thinking to develop a thesis topic. I decided to write something regarding the Black Lives Matter movement. When I read Kee's book, I said to myself that his *argument here is an eye-opening assessment that intellectually insists that Black theology was dead. How is what Kee stated valid for me? I am a Black theologian who has a Black theology, and my theology is not over.*

Next, I read your book, which appeared to be a direct response to Kee. You suggest that spirit or glossolalia in the Pentecostal Church is a valid reply to Kee. However, I am interested in knowing what the Black Pentecostal Church in Britain has done or is doing to obtain public policy changes for Black people and or those dispossessed citizens of Great Britain.

So, considering your book, I realized it was more than an infatuation with Alistair Kee's argument for two reasons. First, your book was written to demonstrate that you believe that a political theology represents the heart and soul of the Black Pentecostal Church in Britain. Second, your book provides me with the impetus and desire to write a political theology for the Black Lives Matter movement.

Robert Beckford: Nonviolent Direct Action to Achieve Reparations

You probably already know what I am about to say. However, the request for reparation to compensate the people of the African diaspora is nothing new. Before The Poor People's March on Washington and Martin Luther King Jr.'s tragic assassination, he insisted that reparations are nothing new in America. When the White Americans were moving out to western states, the American government gave away land to them. Also, the American government periodically pays farmers subsidies not to farm products. So, King promised that when they went to Washington DC for the march, they would ask that our government give us our overdue check. United States Representative John Conyers Jr. was elected to serve the people of Michigan for over fifty years. Every year, he submitted a resolution for the American government to pay reparations to African Americans.

Likewise, you prepared a video called *The Empire Pays Back*. I listened carefully to it and watched it on YouTube. It was thought-provoking. Admittedly, your presentation was also highly informative. Based on your extensive research, you revealed that Britain owed the victims of the Atlantic slave trade approximately 7.5 trillion pounds.

I have decided likewise to compose a letter to you because I want to understand your thoughts and reflections about how to obtain reparations for African Americans. Since nonviolent direct action was used strategically to secure voting rights for African Americas, do you believe that nonviolent direct action should be used also to obtain reparations for those of the African diaspora?

Chapter 2

MY FAMILY HERITAGE: FIGHTERS FOR JUSTICE AND EQUALITY

Silas Clayton Sr. (PaPa), My Grandfather

My fraternal grandfather, Silas Clayton Sr., whom we affectionately called PaPa, lived to be 107 years of age. He was born at the beginning of the nineteenth century in Lake Cormorant, Mississippi. He had several siblings, including Aunt Viola Clayton-Miller, Aunt Sweet, Uncle Clayborne, Uncle Ben, Uncle Joe, and Uncle Odell (Kid). Joe Rucker PaPa's father, died at an early age. Papa's grandfather, Aaron Clayton, raised him from a young age until he became a grown man. Papa's formal education was minimal. He advised me, "Son, I was only allowed to complete the seventh grade. I attended school at my one-room church, Counts Chapel Color (Christian) Methodist Church (CCCM)."

The CCCM congregation remains a socially and politically engaged congregation. The CCCM mission statement insists the church exists as "a transforming church for Jesus the Christ within a changing world." The church believes "the Christian religion doth not prohibit, but that a man may swear when the magistrate required, in a cause of faith and charity, so it is done according to the prophet's teaching, injustice, judgment, and truth."

PaPa did not obtain his high school diploma, but he always encouraged his children, grandchildren, and everyone he met to receive the best education possible. I remember him continually saying that education is a short-term sacrifice for long-term gain. Now, I also came to understand that PaPa's positive attitude regarding education was an attitude that was reflected throughout my community.

I became a Christian believer at the New Nonconnah Missionary Baptist Church (NNMB) at ten years of age. To become a member of the church, I said my ABCs. I **a**ccepted Christ into my life. I came to **b**elieve in Jesus Christ. I **c**onfessed my hope and belief in Jesus Christ. I also informed PaPa about my confession of faith and that I had accepted Christ into my life. He asked me to explain how I had come to Christ.

I said, "PaPa, recently, I attended Vacation Bible School at NNMBC. The bus driver, Reverend Robert Lee Jones, picked us up for two weeks. He picked up my brothers, cousins, friends, and me for VBS and took us to church. After VBS class, we were provided a delicious lunch in the NNMBC fellowship hall. Reverend Jones also conducted a revival service and invited Reverend Lawson, the pastor of Middle Baptist Church, to serve as the evangelist. You know Reverend Lawson is one of those whopping, hollering, singing preachers. After completing his sermon, Reverend Lawson had all of us on the mourner's bench who had accepted Christ's step forward. I did what Pastor Lawson asked of me. I told him that I had accepted Christ into my life."

Papa said, "Son, that is all you did? You did not shout and give praise to God that you have become a believer?"

"No, PaPa. I did not shout or make any noise. I just told Reverend Lawson I accepted Christ as my Lord and Savior. PaPa insisted, "Well, son, you have no religion. You got to go back on the mourner's bench because, when you get religion, I believe you have to feel something. You got to shout off the mourner's bench."

Since I wanted to do what PaPa requested, I could hardly wait to attend the NNMBC worship service. When Reverend Jones had his next NNMBC worship service, I did precisely what PaPa asked me to do. I intentionally began to shout and give praise to God.

Pastor Jones was our longtime minister. Previously, he had performed my parents' marriage ceremony. Like me, they were also members of NNMBC. But, like so many Black preachers, he was an uneducated minister. Despite being ill-prepared educationally, he always encouraged his congregation to pursue a formal education as far as possible.

PaPa repeatedly told us about our family history: "When my grandmother died, granddaddy Aaron married my schoolteacher, Ms. Alice. She was part Indian. The fact Ms. Alice was part Indian is nothing strange; all of us know that America is nothing but a cultural melting pot of mixed races."

In the Lake Cormorant community, there was no school beyond the seventh grade for Black children to attend. They attended school no more than six to seven months yearly.

They spent their other time chopping, picking, or working in the fields.

Nonetheless, because of limited educational opportunities in Lake Cormorant, PaPa suggested that his Granddaddy Aaron send him to Memphis to live with relatives, which enabled him to attend a few years at the LeMoyne Normal School. (It is now called LeMoyne-Owen College. Years later, I was able to participate in and graduate from LeMoyne-Owen College.)

I once asked PaPa which relative he lived with in Memphis during his student days at LeMoyne. He replied, "Son, my cousin was named Reverend Thompson. He served as the pastor of Central Baptist Church. Sadly, Reverend Thompson and another preacher friend both drowned during a fishing trip in Arkansas."

"Wow! PaPa, I can't believe that. I'm now an associated minister at Central Baptist Church on Joubert Avenue. The Reverend Dr. Reuben H. Green is now the senior pastor. Several years ago, Pastor Green ordained and licensed me."

What PaPa stated about religion, and specifically the Black church, was somewhat intertwined with my life, living, and purpose for living. Because of my calling and preparation for ministry, I have been allowed to serve our nation in the military and travel the world. Also, my life reminds me that the church remains the most potent and enduring institution within the Black community. But the question remains: How can we use this collective power to create a stronger community and nation?

PaPa eventually relocated from Memphis to Saint Louis, Missouri. There, he lived with his brother, Odell (Uncle Kid). He worked various jobs to support himself; however, his grandfather and my great-great-grandfather, Aaron Clayton, were ill and could not farm and care for the family property in Mississippi. At that time, PaPa met and married Robelia Saulsberry. (PaPa affectionately called her Bloss, but her children and grandchildren called her Momma.) Momma and her family were Mount Olive Missionary Baptist Church (MOMBC) members in Nesbit, Mississippi. After their marriage, PaPa transferred his church membership from CCCMC to MOMBC. They had fourteen children and a host of grandchildren and great-grandchildren. Later, I asked PaPa, "Why did you transfer your membership to MOMBC?"

He said, "Bloss and I agreed that if we married, I would transfer membership to MOMBC. It was critically important that we cooperated and worked together in everything we did." "Now, PaPa, I have spent many days and nights with you and Momma at your house, and I have noticed that you and Momma discipline your children, especially your grandchildren, differently. You use mostly verbal communication when you discipline. For instance, if I have done something you disagree with, you typically say, 'Son, I am disappointed with you because I thought you had better sense than that.' On the other hand, Momma has advised and talked with me when I have done wrong. She let me know. However, unlike you, Momma also believes what the Bible says—spare the rod and spoil the child. Momma has never disciplined me with one of her leather belts, but I have seen her use her belt on my Uncle June Boy and other cousins."

PaPa replied, "Son, everybody is different. God made us different. Bloss and I are different in how we discipline young children."

Aaron Clayton: My Great-Great-Grandfather

PaPa reminded me endlessly that my great-great-grandfather, Aaron Clayton, was born into slavery somewhere in South Carolina. When President Abraham Lincoln signed the Emancipation Proclamation, Aaron, like all slaves, received his freedom. At the time of emancipation, Aaron was a young teenager who did not know where his parents, siblings, and other family members were. He, therefore, began to wander from plantation to plantation and from place to place, trying to eke out an existence. He ended up in Desoto County in Northern Mississippi and worked on the shores of the Mississippi River, loading and unloading ships. He was extremely frugal in terms of saving his money. At his death, Aaron, an illiterate, formerly enslaved person, left nearly two hundred acres of land to his children and grandchildren.

I have often thought about how a formerly enslaved person could amass so much property when he was unable to read or write. Maybe this old saying, "God is a miracle worker," has some value and validity, particularly when the believer believes it.

PaPa's story about Aaron Clayton intuitively shaped my understanding of my family, theology, religion, and history and helped me to develop a philosophy of religion long before I could read or write. As a student at Booker T. Washington High School, I took a course in American history. At that time, the content of the course seemed familiar because I had learned so much of it already through the countless history discussions with my grandfather and then other talks, I'd had with other senior family members and church members. This enabled me eventually to develop a political theology. My political theology reflects what I have seen in the civil rights movement, specifically under the leadership of Martin Luther King Jr. He served as the dynamic leader of the Southern Christian Leadership Conference (SCLC). In his political theology, he believed that God is always involved with us and our people in our struggle to obtain our freedom through nonviolent direct actions in America and worldwide.

About four years after the Brown v. Board of Education of Topeka decision, Elizabeth Murphy-Clayton, my beloved mother, began a daily routine to prepare me for my first school days. She took me through what I call the Elizabeth Early School Boot Camp. Among other things, this consisted of her teaching me the ABCs and teaching me to count from one hundred to one thousand. Although she was loving and devoted, my mother was also a kind of drill sergeant. If I could not recite my ABCs correctly or count appropriately, she punished me accordingly. If I recited ABD instead of ABC, I received the anguish of my mother in the form of a hit on my hand or arm along with the admonition, "It is A-B-*C* and not A-B-*D*."

Momma Elizabeth took me to get immunized before I started as a first grader at Geeter Elementary School. My father, Otis (Aaron) Clayton Sr., dropped us off at John Gaston Hospital before he went to work that morning. Later that afternoon, I obtained my immunizations. My mother and I boarded the Memphis City bus to travel back home. This was the time of the evening rush hour when people were getting off from their various jobs. We were seated in the middle section of the bus. This was during the dark days of legal segregation and legal discrimination.

Even then, I looked forward to the day when I and my people would not face this kind of dehumanization. I had heard these ideas even as a child. They are expressed in the Declaration of Independence, "We hold these truths to be self-evident all men are created by their creator with certain unalienable rights, and among these are life, liberty, and the pursuit of happiness." But, on that day, those words did not apply to us. My mother and I had to get up from our seats and give them over to a White man. She held me in her arms as we traveled home on the Memphis City Bus.

I attended the Memphis public schools until I graduated from Booker T. Washington High School. Throughout my years in public school, several excellent teachers impacted and influenced me—Mr. Carroll, Mrs. Wakefield, and Coach Harold Macrae. Mr. Carroll and Mrs. Wakefield were my sixth-grade teachers at Geeter Elementary School.

Mr. Carroll was, I believe, a former member of the military and a Prince Hall Masonic Member like my father. Mr. Carroll may have been injured during his military service. He had a prosthetic leg and walked with a limp. I decided to wear my Daddy's red Masonic ring to school one day. I showed it off to my classmates. Then, one of them said, "Mr. Carroll, have you seen Otis's red ring?" He remarked, "Otis, son, let me see your red ring." I took it off my left middle finger and showed it to him. Mr. Carroll then insisted, "Otis, I am sorry, but I must keep your ring.

You must tell your father that I have it. He must come to school and get it from me."

My Daddy came home from work later that evening. I told him, "Daddy, Mr. Carroll took your ring from me today. He has it and says you need to visit the school so you can retrieve it."

"Puddin," he replied, "you had no business taking my ring. Did you take it out of my dresser drawer?" Yes, Daddy replied, "You must stay out of my belongings. I will go to your school tomorrow morning on my way to work to get my ring."

I learned from that experience that Mr. Carroll was more than likely also a Masonic brother and that becoming a Mason had some apparent political and social meaning and significance. In my more mature years, I also became a member of the local lodge and the brotherhood.

Later, in my sixth year of public school, Mr. Carroll became severely ill and was unable to return to school. Mrs. Wakefield became my teacher for the remainder of the year. I know that no two people are the same, but Mrs. Wakefield's behavior and manner of teaching were diametrically different from Mr. Carroll's. I began to rebel and skip school. Some days, I would steal some of my Daddy's corn whiskey and take it to school to share with some classmates—Sam Turner, Billy Hightower, and Curtis Golden. On other days, we would go into the woods, ride horses, swing in the trees, and swim rather than enter Mrs. Wakefield's classroom. My grades dropped, and I was briefly suspended from school.

My mother, Elizabeth, informed Luther Murphy, her father, and my grandfather about my school suspension and behavior. His grandchildren called him Granddaddy. He was hardworking and provided for his family's needs and wants. He farmed cotton on his property across the state line in Horn Lake, Mississippi. Additionally, at night, Granddaddy worked for Firestone Tire and Rubber.

Most importantly, like PaPa, he was also a devoted Christian who worked faithfully in the Nonconnah Baptist Church. But, unlike PaPa, Granddaddy was a strict disciplinarian who believed that sparing the rod spoils the child. He used a leather belt and an extension cord for his discipline.

So, one night after getting off from work, Grandaddy stopped by our home to offer me some of his discipline medicine. Before beating me with the extension cord, he said, "I hear you have been acting a fool at school. You are now suspended. But I want to remind you that no child or grandchild has ever been suspended from school. You are stubborn and hardheaded. Now I got something, especially for you."

After that beating from Granddaddy, I was never suspended from school. I continued, however, to have trouble adjusting to Mrs. Wakefield's teaching methods. Sadly, I repeated the sixth grade. I did learn an invaluable lesson: Sometimes, children, like adults, can become traumatized by sudden, unexpected changes in their routines. I was bothered by the shift from Mr. Carroll to Mrs. Wakefield. Additionally, at that time, the deteriorating relationship between my parents was affecting me emotionally and psychologically. They were arguing, and fighting increased in the presence of me and my siblings in our home.

When I think about my last years in public school, Coach Harold Macrae quickly comes to mind. He was also a Booker T. Washington High School graduate from the historically Black Lane College in Jackson, Tennessee, where he was a member of the Omega Psi Phi Fraternity and a devoted leader in his church. He was my basketball coach during my sophomore year.

Now, after that season, I learned that my mother had hurt both of her hands while working at her dangerous manufacturing job at the Memphis Furniture Company. I needed to secure a full-time job to care for my mother and eight siblings financially. Although I was a high school student, I was blessed to secure a full-time night job at the Southern Central Paper Company. I worked from three in the afternoon until eleven at night during the week and often worked overtime on weekends.

Although I no longer played basketball, Coach Macrae said, "Clayton, I understand that you may not be playing basketball for Booker T. Washington High School, but you are still a student here. I see something in you. I think you can make something out of your life. Sadly, you're running around and keeping the wrong company since you no longer play basketball. I see you with some of your friends who don't mean you any good. So, from now on, I will adopt you as my son. If you get into any trouble, I want you to know that I will deal with you accordingly. You kick my ass. Or I will kick your ass. I say this to you because I must remind you that you are a Black male teenager, and the police are waiting for you to do something stupid. And, when you do, they will then lock you up in the jailhouse and throw away the key. So, it is my responsibility to help you make the right and most prudent decisions."

As things turned out, Coach McCrae and I had several verbal and physical altercations. One evening after school, my friends and I were hanging out. We were standing on the corner of Mississippi and Walker outside the famous Four Way Grill Restaurant and Heavy's Pool Hall. Mr. Bugeye Johnson, the assistant principal at Booker T. Washington, drove by and stopped at the red light. He saw me, and I saw him; we made eye contact. I was not on the school campus. The school was not in session, and I did not like Mr. Johnson or care anything about him. Maybe I simply had an iconoclastic attitude toward his authority or leadership style. I began to shout obscenities and curse words at Bugeye Johnson. "You fat, ugly motherfucker! You ugly son of a bitch!"

My friends and I all laughed uncontrollably. My friends remarked, "Crookedhead, you know, you are crazy and hell. Hahahaha!" Crookedhead was my street name in the hood. Everyone in the hood had a nickname. Terry Murchison, a friend and fellow basketball player, gave me that name. Terry said, "Each time you shoot the basketball, you crook your head to the side." Thus, Terry and everyone on the street called me "Crookedhead." Without saying a word to me, Bugeye Johnson drove away from the light and continued to his destination.

I arrived at school the following day and went to my homeroom, where I checked in before classes began. Mr. Springer, the principal, made his traditional morning announcements over the public address system. Immediately after those announcements, Mr. Springer stated, "Otis

Clayton, you must report to my office right now. If you do not report to my office, you will be suspended. Your parents will then have to take you to the Memphis City School Board of Education for readmission."

I reported to Mr. Springer's office, and he took me into his office. Presenters were Mr. Springer, Mr. Johnson, and Coach Macrae. Mr. Springer said, "Clayton, I understand that you and your friends were on the corner of Mississippi and Walker yesterday when Mr. Johnson drove by. He stopped at the corner. You were the ringleader. Mr. Johnson says that you hurled profanities and obscenities at him. If you did that, your behavior is not becoming a student here at this school. What do you have to say in your defense?"

"Mr. Springer, I said something like that to Mr. Johnson. I do not recall using profanity and curse words, but I was not here on the school property regardless of what was said to him. I was on the corner of Mississippi and Walker." Then Mr. Springer said, "Mr. Johnson, Coach Macrae, do you have anything to say to our student?"

Mr. Johnson said, "Son, I do not appreciate what you and your friends said. This must not happen again. Clayton, do you understand that?" I replied, "Yes, sir."

Coach Macrae said, "Mr. Springer and Mr. Johnson, this young man, Otis Clayton, was once one of my basketball players here at school. He does not play basketball here now, but he knows me, and I know him. I have adopted Clayton as one of my sons. I told him he must stop hanging out with some of his thug friends. But, if you do not mind, after Mr. Johnson disciplines him, I need to talk to my son alone in my office in the gym."

Mr. Springer addressed me, "Do you agree to take the discipline from Mr. Johnson and Coach Macrae? If you don't, I will suspend you from Booker T. Washington, and your parents must travel to the Board of Education to get you readmitted."

I said, "Yes, sir" immediately. I certainly did not want my mother to go through all that. She was already dealing with her medical issues and household issues. So, I took three licks on my rear end from Mr. Bugeye Johnson.

Then, I walked with Coach Macrae to his office in the gym. He took off his suit coat and necktie and stood before me, looking into my eyes. Then he repeated something he had said to me previously: "Son, I see something in you. I asked you to stop fucking around with those thugs in the street. They do not mean you any good. If you do not do that, you are on your way to jail, or you will die an early death. I do not want it to happen to you. Now, you kick my ass, or I am going to kick your ass." So, we wrestled back and forth for about five minutes or so. I was not a physical match for Coach Macrae. Oh, yes, I was six foot two, but I weighed only about 140 pounds. Coach Macrae was also six foot two and weighed nearly 240 pounds. After our fight, he said, "You are my son. I see something in you." He hugged me. We both shed a few tears, and he gave me a written excuse to join my next class a bit late.

The following school year, Coach Macrae became a school administrator; his new position was principal at Westwood High School. The years went by so quickly. During those years, I often thought of Coach Macrae's interest in me. I decided to make a surprise visit to Westwood High School to visit with him. I walked into the main office wearing my green, heavily starched United States Army uniform and my military-issued shiny polished combat boots. I informed the security and office staff members, "I am Major Otis Clayton, and I was one of Principal Harold Macrae's adopted sons. I haven't seen him in nearly thirty years. Tell him that I have dropped by his school for a brief visit." Principal Macrae came out of his office and embraced me. He told his office staff and everyone present, "Look here, everybody. This is one of my adopted sons. I coached, taught, and mentored him at Booker T. Washington High School. God has kept his hands on him. I am so proud of him."

I honestly believe that it is primarily to never give up on people. If we are alive, God is not through with us yet. When God gets through with us, we shall become like pure gold.

It was not until my sophomore year of high school that the desegregation of public schools personally impacted me. I became a student of my first White American educators: a White female homeroom teacher and a White male coach-teacher.

The Emmett Till Murder and Trial. Emmett Till was a fourteen-year-old Black boy who was murdered in 1955 in a racist attack. At the time of his death, I was only three years of age. My parents had three children, and a fourth child, my sister Faye, was due to be born within the next few months. When my Daddy got home from work each evening, he immediately called out to me, his firstborn. I was his namesake, Otis, Jr., but he called me by my nickname—Puddin. "Puddin, come here," he would call out. I would sit with his arms around me while we watched the CBS evening news featuring Walter Cronkite. My Daddy always seemed to have an interest in what was going on in the world. Shortly after that, my Momma, Elizabeth, would bring him dinner. He would eat and feed me some of his dinner.

Uncle John Henry Ray lived next door to us and was married to Rosie Lee (Aunt Dump). Uncle John Henry worked for a local fuel company. And, if he were not working overtime, he would always drop by. He and Daddy discussed what was going on within their Masonic order and current events. The Emmet Till Murder and trial was just one of many events they talked about. I heard Uncle John Henry say, "Boy, Otis. This killing of that small Boy from Chicago down in Money, Mississippi, was simply awful, terrible, and deeply sad. I hear that the NAACP, the Urban League, and the FBI are involved in finding out what happened to the little lad, Emmett Till. I know it is nothing but those low-down, dirty Klansmen who were involved in his abduction and death. I believe we in our Masonic Lodge need to do something."

My father, Otis (or Boy as family members and close friends him), Uncle Henry, and other men they were friends with were not church members. They were, however, diehard supporters of social and political causes. This speaks to the need for local congregations to be socially and politically engaged in social justice.

Rosa Parks & The Montgomery Bus Boycott. I feel reasonably confident that the success of the Montgomery Bus Boycott greatly impacted political and social changes in the city of Memphis. The Memphis Transit Authority decided to employ Black bus drivers. Reverend Keith Whalum was hired as the first Black bus driver. His family background was impressive. His family had been part owners of the historic Black-owned Metropolitan Insurance Company. Reverend Whalum's mother was a former Memphis school teacher and educator. He had attended Tennessee State University and served honorably in the United States Air Force.

Reverend Whalum was later appointed to become human resources director for the United States Post Office in Memphis. This gave him tremendous power to employ and hire more African Americans. During the summer of 1968, my dear friend, James Tojo Smith, informed me that Reverend Whalum had hired him. He said, "Crookethead, if you want a summer job, I suggest that that go down to see Reverend Whalum at the post office."

I followed Tojo's instructions and advice. I immediately went to Reverend Whalum's office and told his White female secretary, "Ma'am, I'm here to see him. I'm a student at Booker T. Washington and deeply interested in summer employment."

She responded, "I am sorry, but Reverend Whalum is not seeing anyone today." I said, "Ma'am, I know what you just said, but I can see Reverend Whalum right now through the window behind you". Again, she said, "Young man, I'm sorry, but Reverend Whalum is not seeing anyone today."

I thanked her, but I stepped outside of Reverend Whalum's office. *This summer job could help me, my mother, and my siblings.* Then I thought, *I can see Reverend Whalum. He is in the office right behind the secretary's office. What the hell with this shit! The hell with what that* White *secretary said. I need a summer job for my family.*

I walked back into the personnel office, past the White secretary's desk, and entered Reverend Whalum's office. His White secretary came running behind me. She said, "Reverend Whalum, I told him you were not seeing anyone."

I said, "Reverend Whalum, sir. Please. I need a summer job for my mom, siblings, and me. "Reverend Whalum said to his secretary, "He's okay. I got him. Can you please leave and pull the door closed behind you?" Then, Reverend Whalum remarked, "Son, can you tell me something about yourself?"

"Yes, sir. I am happy to tell you something about me. I am a junior at Booker T. Washington High School. I have ambitions to graduate and go on to college somewhere. But, right now, I need a summer job to help my Momma provide for my siblings." "Now, I am delighted you know how to express yourself," Reverend Whalum remarked. "Can you start working at the Crosstown Post Office tomorrow morning?" "Yes, sir. I can start tomorrow morning. Reverend Whalum, I thank you from the depths of my heart for helping me."

I worked at the Crosstown Post Office throughout the summer. I made more money than I had made in my entire life. That summer income made our lives more bearable. I met many employees who were civil servants and veterans. They took me under their wings and gave me the wisdom, knowledge, and understanding to live better. In short, the success of the Montgomery Bus Protest benefitted me, other African Americans, and people across America.

Civil Rights Act of 1964. I was not present at the March on Washington in 1963. Still, I listened attentively to the news and experienced the event vicariously through the experience of the Reverend Dr. Martin Luther King, Jr. Reverend King, like me, was a Baptist preacher who delivered his monumental, powerful, and soul-stirring speech called "I Have a Dream."

Also, I lived vicariously through the experience of Frederick (or Freddie) Williams, my brother-in-law. He was there to hear Dr. King and to experience this wonderful, historic occasion. At that time, Freddie was only eleven years of age, but he had traveled there with friends and supporters from Memphis, Tennessee. They were members of the civil rights movement who took him and other youths nationwide to the march. This event inspired Freddie ultimately to serve America by going into the military. He asked his parents, at the tender age of seventeen before graduating from high school, to sign for him so that he could volunteer to become a member of the United States Navy.

Moreover, while in the Navy, he earned his high school diploma. Freddie also provided over twenty years of service to God and his country in the military. The Civil Rights Act of 1964 was passed mainly because of the pressure the civil rights marches placed on elected officials to do something about African Americans' right to vote and take advantage of economic opportunities. I clearly understand that there had been at least two other Civil Rights Act legislations, 1866 and 1875.

So, I asked why Congress does not just go ahead and codify civil rights, particularly the right to vote. This appeared to be the most prudent and rational thing to do.

It would benefit all Americans for everyone to have the right to vote for the candidate of their choice. But I know that codifying the right to vote is not easy. Right now, the Republicans and those especially who make up the United States Supreme Court are seeking to take away any woman's right to have an abortion. Given this sad reality, I share the opinion, strategy, and tactically to employ nonviolent direction to put pressure on Congress to codify both abortion rights and the right to vote. This kind of pressure ultimately led to the Civil Rights Act of 1964. With that same degree of coordination and determination, the voting rights and abortion rights advocates can accomplish and obtain their goals.

Church Bombings in Birmingham, Alabama, and other acts of violence. I believe the bombings of Black churches in Birmingham, Alabama, were nothing new. This was simply one of the same methods that White supremacists and White racists have used to terrify and intimidate Blacks and other people of color throughout American history. My great-great-grandfather Aaron Clayton's life and legacy are in some way a reflection of and a reaction to this demonic attitude and action. Because of that situation, he struggled relentlessly to obtain his liberation, freedom, and bondage from slavery.

Nonetheless, even today, White supremacists and White racists remain on the rampage, stoking fears of a racist ideology replacement theory that Blacks, Jews, and other minorities are trying to destroy and replace them. Subsequently, a young White male supremacist went into the Emmanuel Church in South Carolina and shot and killed

Blacks as they worshipped. Then, another young White supremacist in New York drove nearly four hours upstate from his residence to Buffalo, New York, to a grocery that he had targeted.

So, the church bombing that took place in Birmingham, Alabama, is just one of multiple acts of violence that sadly have been visited upon my people endlessly. I believe that this kind of violence against our people and all people must be brought to an end. Now, this requires members of the church, other religious bodies, people with moral conscience, and elected officials to band together and work toward constructive political solutions.

The church bombings, particularly that of the 16th Street Baptist Church, where four little girls were killed, were almost surreal. This revealed, again and again, the diabolical nature of the White American power structure to disenfranchise and oppress people of color. Donald Trump and his followers quickly come to mind. The White power structure will do, at any time, absolutely anything to keep Black people and the marginalized from achieving their God-given dignity, equality, and justice.

Civil Rights Marches and Protests. On the day that Dr. King came to participate and lead in the Memphis sanitation strike, Mr. Springer made a morning announcement over the public address system: "Young people, like me, you are aware that Dr. Martin Luther King Jr. and members of the Southern Christian Leadership Conference have a protest march downtown. I want all of you to know that you are supposed to be here at Booker T. Washington High School attending your class. Dr. King is himself a highly educated man. Like Dr. King, you need the best and highest education possible to make something out of your life. And we have received word that the Memphis Invaders and some other groups will cause violence to take place at the march."

Dr. King led the march on that day, and violence took place; however, I did not attend the march because I rationalized that it was best that I went to school. Further, I reasoned that if I went to the parade, I could get into trouble and get arrested, and that would cause trauma for me and my family, especially my mother. She would be the one who would have to come to get me out of jail. Momma had already warned me on several occasions. "Puddin, if you ever get into trouble with the police and get yourself arrested, you will be alone. I will not bail you out of jail. I sometimes do not have enough money to put food on the table and pay my bills."

On the evening of April 2, 1968, my father visited the house to visit us. At the time, my parents were going through divorce proceedings. He asked me, "You know Dr. King is returning to town tomorrow evening? There is also supposed to be a thunderstorm tomorrow evening. Are you going to hear Dr. King speak at Clayborne Temple?" "Daddy, I do not know," I said.

Dr. King arrived the next day at the Memphis International Airport. Reverend Reuben Green, my pastor, served as his driver and was there at the airport to pick him up and drive him directly to the Loraine Hotel. It was raining heavily that evening; there was a thunderstorm warning. So, it was believed that the crowd at Clayborne Temple would be small, but on the contrary, it was vast. The crowd at the church was busting at the seams; therefore, despite the thunderstorm warning, a large crowd of civil rights supporters for the sanitation workers came to hear Dr. King speak. He gave his final oration, "I Have Been to the Mountaintop," at the historic Church of God in Christ, Clayborne Temple.

Dr. King was assassinated the next evening while standing on the balcony of his Lorraine Hotel room. His assassination, in my estimation, has forever tarnished the moral reputation of the city of Memphis. It is the city where people conspired to kill Dr. Martin Luther King Jr, one of our nation's great leaders. It is my belief that even members of the clergy, who were envious of his powerful influence and leadership, were involved in some way in Dr. King's assassination.

However, within days after King's death, the mayor of Memphis and the Memphis City Council agreed to end the Memphis sanitation strike and give the sanitation workers an increase in wages and other benefits. Now, I have learned something subsequently from civil rights marches and protests. It is the realization essentially that an altruistic philosophy will always ultimately yield positive benefits. Like our ancestors, Dr. King gave his life serving others through the power of love, self-sacrifice, and fighting against social evils. His intellectual and spiritual insights are surely a guiding light for positive social and political change.

Election of Barack Obama as President. Reverend Jessie Jackson and I have much in common. We are both members of the clergy in the Baptist tradition, graduates of a historically Black college and believe that the church and faith traditions must be involved socially and politically.

This is how political progress and change take place in a democracy.

When Reverend Jackson decided to become a candidate for the United States presidency, he inspired and electrified Blacks and other minorities to run for public office. It was then that I also made the decision to seek public office. I became a candidate for an at-large Memphis City Council seat. Eight other candidates who were more famous citizens of Memphis were running for this seat. They included household names in the city of Memphis, like Minerva Jernigan, Janice Hooks, and Reverend Kenneth Whalum. Minerva Jernigan was a former longtime member of the Memphis City Council. Janice Hooks was married to Michael Hooks, who was the Shelby County property assessor. Also, because of her marriage to Michael Hooks, she was the niece of the renowned clergy, pastor, lawyer, and judge Benjamin Hooks. Reverend Kenneth Whalum was the former human resource manager for the local United States Post Office, the Olivet Missionary Baptist Church pastor, and the father of the world-renowned musician Kirk Whalum.

Because none of us obtained enough votes to become victorious, the Shelby County Election Commission held a runoff between the candidates who had received the most votes. These two candidates were Janice Hooks and Reverend Kenneth Whalum. Consequently, I was completely caught by surprise. One morning, Michael Hooks, Janice's husband, called and asked, "Reverend Clayton, how are you doing? You know my wife Janice is in the runoff with Reverend Whalum. I want to know if you could give her your support." I replied, "Michael, man, I am sorry, but

Reverend Whalum, like me, is a preacher and member of the clergy. I decided to give him my support."

Reverend Whalum became victorious by becoming the at-large city councilman. But, honestly, I must admit that running for public office took me away from my family and my calling to serve as a minister and pastor. So, I have decided that I will no longer seek public office. I have learned and realized that every politician and even the president needs a devoted pastor to offer them spiritual advice and support.

I was pleasantly surprised and yet amazed that Barack Obama became the first African American and person of color elected as the president of the United States of America. I did believe that one day, America would elect a person of color as president, but I did not think it would occur within my lifetime. I guess I had not given it much thought since I was interested primarily in securing the best education possible to become an influential Baptist preacher who used the power of eloquence to get things accomplished for my congregation and all of God's people.

Since Obama was elected as president, I have taken time to reflect on what he was able to accomplish. I am confident it was through the love, grace, and mercy of God that Obama received the love and support of his family and others within the larger American society for him to become president. Like me, Obama prepared himself for leadership. He worked endlessly to complete high school, college, and law school and volunteered to become a public servant.

When Obama became a candidate for president for the first time, I supported him from the sidelines by voting for him and encouraging my family members and friends to do likewise.

During his second campaign for president, I left Memphis, Tennessee, and relocated to Denver, Colorado, for gainful employment. I accepted a position within the Department of Veteran Affairs. At that time, I also became more engaged in union activities and became actively inspired by Obama's reelection campaign. I became a leader and participant in the Leadership Circle of Colorado, which was a group of progressive Democrats who worked, campaigned, and raised money for Obama. More specifically, I became a veteran for Obama, speaking to and motivating other veterans across America, their family members, and their friends, convincing them why we needed to reelect President Obama."

When he was reelected, I expressed an interest to serve in any manner as an appointee in the Barack Obama/Joe Biden administration, but I was not asked to serve. For the most part, I supported most of the administration's policies, specifically those related to healthcare and support for veterans and their families.

Election of Kamala Harris as Vice President. Without hesitation or equivocation, I was extremely excited and delighted that Kamala Harris became the first woman and person of color to be elected vice president. I support equal opportunity and equal pay for all women, including minorities.

I met former United States Senator Kamala Harris several years ago in Ashen, Colorado. Senator Harris addressed the Colorado gathering to support fundraising and other

Democratic state and national agenda concerns. But, during most of the Joe Bidden/Kamala Harris campaign to win the White House, I supported their campaign as a veteran and a fundraiser. In May 2020, I had a virtual meeting with Vice President Joe Bidden and United States Senator Corey Booker. In that meeting, Senator Booker, who served as the facilitator, introduced me to Vice President Bidden. Although I did not request that he provide a position, I expressed my interest by asking that Bidden recruit highly qualified veterans to serve in his presidential administration.

I informed him of something my devoted mother, Elizabeth Murphy-Clayton, requested that I mention. She had told me, "Please let Bidden know that I will be glad when he wins the office of the president so that he can put Trump's ass out of the White House. I am sick and tired of seeing Trump. He is only concerned about himself and not the American people." I agree with my mother's assessment because the Bidden/Harris administration seeks to enact, with the help of God, concerned citizens, and the United States Congress, the "Build Back Better" initiative for the American people.

Black Lives Matter Movement (BLM). I became especially interested in the Black Lives Matter movement while involved in post-doctoral studies at Canterbury Christ University in England. In the process, I learned that the BLM, as a movement, reflects more of what African Americans and other oppressed members of America are seeking, namely, justice, fairness, and economic equality. Unlike most movements in the Black community, the BLM movement did not begin within the African-American religious community.

When I returned to America from England, I attended several local BLM meetings in Nashville, Tennessee. At each meeting, I let those in attendance know that I had been referred by Ashley King, who was a member, but he was never present. At each meeting, I was asked what pronouns I wished people to use when referring to me. I told them they could use he/him. I understand that the founders of the BLM are LGBTQ-sensitive.

I have been aware that there have always been members of the church who were LGBTQ oriented. I became the pastor of my first congregation at the Antioch Missionary Baptist Church (AMBC) in Batesville, Mississippi. It was the oldest Black congregation in the city. Although it was located in the rural section of Batesville, I had approximately seven hundred thunders to a thousand members. I did not know that I had that many members until trouble started.

Under my leadership, AMBBC had begun to grow. The congregation agreed and voted that we needed a musician every Sunday, not every other Sunday. The current musician, known to be LGBTQ, had already been performing at AMBC before I became the pastor. Although I became aware of his sexual orientation, I had no problem with him, but his schedule allowed him to be present for worship services only every other Sunday. So, when I chaired the church meeting to employ an every-Sunday musician, the LGBTQ musician was voted out. It had nothing to do with his sexual orientation.

Nonetheless, one of my church deacons became upset with me. Now, my point here is that, in the church, historically the Black church, LGBTQ issues and concerns are known, but they are not discussed. BLM is not necessarily a religious organization. But, unlike the Black church, it is open and honest about LGBTQ acknowledgment.

The Riot on January 6, 2021. My fraternal uncles, Ernest Clayton, and Edward (Jack) Clayton, served in a distinguished and honorable manner in the United States Army in World War II. My second cousin, Vola Miller, served in combat on several tours in Vietnam as a noncommissioned officer in the United States Marines. After over twenty years of wearing the military uniform, he retired and spent his remaining years with his devoted wife, Virginia, and their children, readjusting from military to civilian life. Edward Earl Clayton was seventeen when he graduated from Booker T. Washington High School. So, our parents, Elizabeth, and Aaron (Otis), signed for him to enlist in the United States Air Force. After graduating from LeMoyne Owen College and getting married to my high school sweetheart, I volunteered for service in the United States Air Force. Also, my younger brothers, Rickey, Terry, and La Shun served in the Army and Air Force. After servicing for over twenty years, we retired. But, most importantly, my brothers and all our family members served superbly for God and the country. Oh Yes! We put our lives in harm's way to serve our great nation. We are strong and proud African American men but also patriotic Americans who love America. The majestic and magical words of "The Star Spangled Banner" speak to my heart:

O say, can you see
By the dawn's early light
What so proudly we hail'd
At the twilight's last gleaming?
Whose broad stripes and bright stars
Through the difficult fight
O'er the ramparts we watch'd
Were so gallantly streaming?
And the rocket's red glare
The bombs bursting in the air
Gave proof through the night
That our flag was still there
O say, does that star-spangled banner yet wave
O'er the land of the free
And the home of the brave?

Now, I must say, without equivocation or hesitation, that I think what happened on January 6, 2021, was despicable and a mockery to every veteran who has lived and died in service to our nation. The twice-impeached former president, Donald Trump, encouraged and inspired this anti-democratic effort. He demonstrated that he categorically rejected the American people's November 2020 votes, wishes, will, and desires. But the American people should not have been surprised by his actions. Throughout his presidency, Trump clearly illustrated that he wanted to become a dictator or an autocrat. His best friends are dictators like the Russian president, Vladimir Putin. We all know that birds of the feather flock together.

Since the January insurrection event, I believe Trump, his allies, and the supporters of this riot must be held accountable for crimes committed against the American people. America's understanding of democracy is on trial and under attack. This is a democracy that I love. I consistently revealed my love for America by proudly wearing the United States of America Army uniform for more than twenty years. I volunteered for the sake of American democracy and values to constantly place my life in harm's way in service to God and country.

To help save and secure American democracy, I firmly insist that the following things must occur: (1) A select, or special committee of the United States Congress must be appointed to investigate the January 6, 2021, riot at the United States Capitol, and (2) the United States Department of Justice must direct the Federal Bureau of Investigation (FBI) to ensure that all responsible parties involved in the January 6 riot are held accountable. They ultimately must stand before the seat of justice for their criminal acts and be prosecuted accordingly.

Yes! I will forever remain thankful for Papa's story about his grandfather, Aaron Clayton. I have internalized Papa's story within my bosom and my entire being. In other words, Papa's story has become my own story. I have used it as a steppingstone and foundation for understanding our world and how I must respond to it as a descendant of enslaved African Americans. John Perry Sr. served as a deacon when I was a member of Central Baptist Church in Memphis, Tennessee.

Additionally, John volunteered to become my campaign manager when campaigning to fill the at-large Memphis City Council seat. Like me, he graduated from Booker T. Washington and LeMoyne Owen College and grew up in the ghettos of South Memphis. After I lost that election campaign, John asked, "Reverend Clayton, do you plan to campaign again for public office?"

"Deacon Perry", I remarked, "I no longer have any interest whatsoever in campaigning again for public office. The only thing I am interested in now is campaigning for the Lord and developing a comprehensive strategy to help bring about progressive public policy changes to benefit not the classes but also the masses".

Chapter 3

MY LETTER TO MY OLDEST GRANDSON: A HISTORY OF THE PREACHER IN OUR FAMILY

I want you to know that I am rather excited about what you are doing with your life. You are a single young man approaching your mid-twenties. You are gainfully employed working for the FedEx Corporation in Memphis. Based on our recent conversations, you are primarily interested in continuing to pursue a career with your present employer. It is also inspiring to know that, although you are employed full-time, you are continuing your education as a part-time college student.

But I want to remind you that your employer, FedEx Corporation, has locations worldwide. If you desire, this allows you to relocate and live in different cities. For instance, I worked for FedEx once while living in Memphis, but I was accepted at Vanderbilt University located in Nashville to pursue a doctoral degree. Although I had been accepted as a student at the university, I needed to work because I had a family to support. So, as a FedEx employee, I was able to transfer from Memphis to Nashville. For two years, I worked at night for FedEx and went to school during the day. I completed the course in residence, and four years later, I wrote and submitted my doctoral dissertation to earn my degree from Vanderbilt University.

I want you to understand that you must never become complacent by limiting what you can achieve in life. You must have courage and self-confidence to make the impossible possible. I want you also to share our family history and legacy with family members and friends as I have shared it with you. You are my grandson and also a child of God.

Aunt Ruby

I have known your mother's family for a long time. Long before she was born, I went to Geeter Elementary School with Aunt Ruby. She is one of your mother's sisters. Aunt Ruby and I attended Geeter Elementary School roughly from first to sixth grade. As a student, she always dressed extremely conservatively, pretty dresses, skirts, blouses, coats, and shoes, usually Black, brown, or blue. Aunt Ruby was rather attractive because she had tan skin. Besides her fascinating looks and attire, she was consistently one of my most intelligent classmates; she always made the class and school honor roll. As I recall, Aunt Ruby was voted on and served as a class leader. Although it was kept quiet, she was one of several female classmates I had a crush on. I was in her presence and company regularly because she was the best friend of one of my first cousins, Margaret McGowan.

Annexation

After Ruby completed the sixth grade, the City of Memphis annexed the Alcy Road Community, where Aunt Ruby's family lived. The county school bus that Aunt Ruby and her family members rode to Geeter Elementary School and Geeter High School was terminated. Ruby transferred to Corry Junior High School, within walking distance from her family home. I am sure this created a better comfort zone for Ruby's parents and household because Getter School was located approximately ten miles southwest of Aunt Ruby's home. Still, Corry Junior High School was less than one mile from home. So, if Ruby or one of her sisters became sick or got into difficulties at school, her parents did not have that far to travel. Then, after completing Corry Junior High School, Aunt Ruby attended and graduated from Hamilton High School, which is located less than three miles from home.

LeMoyne Owen College

After Aunt Ruby graduated from Hamilton High School, she and her boyfriend, Jack, got married, and he was drafted to serve in the United States military. Aunt Ruby obtained a job working as a cook in the cafeteria for the Memphis school system. She also began to attend LeMoyne Owen College. When Uncle Jack came home on military leave to spend time with Aunt Ruby, she became pregnant, but it was at LeMoyne Owen College that we reconnected because I was also pursuing a college degree in business with a minor in economics. However, Aunt Ruby did not allow her marriage and having children to impede her dream to pursue higher education. She not only graduated from college with a certification to teach but also obtained her master's degree to become a school principal.

Military Service, Family, and the birth of Your Father.

Immediately after I graduated from LeMoyne, I married your fraternal Grandmother and volunteered for active duty in the United States Air Force. Grandmother, our daughter, and I relocated from Memphis, Tennessee, to Goldsboro, North Carolina, roughly eight hundred miles from Memphis. We were stationed at the Seymour Johnson Air Force Base.

At first, we lived outside the base in a house trailer. This was a challenging period for us. Grandmother Jackie and Auntie Felecia had never traveled or lived that far away from Memphis. Besides being on military duty, I attended graduate school on base at night and on weekends. I was involved in a master of art program with Central Michigan University, which offered an extension graduate school in business management focusing on supervision and business administration. So, the time that I spent with my family was limited. When I was not working, I spent all my available time studying. We lived in Goldsboro for two and half years, and I was transferred to Little Rock Air Force Base in Jacksonville, Arkansas. This was especially significant for many reasons, but mainly because we were now less than 135 miles away from Memphis instead of eight hundred miles away. So, your Grandmother, my family members, and other friends could visit us periodically.

When we moved to Jacksonville, we discovered that Grandmother's first cousin, his wife, and their two children lived there. His mother, Aunt Lois, and your maternal Great-grandmother, Ollie Williams, were sisters. Years earlier, before I met your Grandmother, her first cousin and I attended Porter Junior High. We won the City of Memphis Junior High School Basketball Championship. After completing Porter, we attended different high schools; I went to finish high school at Booker T. Washington, and this cousin (Michael) attended George Washington Carver High School. After graduation, he married his wife, his high school sweetheart, and enlisted in the United States Air Force.

They provided us hospitality, generosity, and kindness as we adjusted the sights and scenes of Jacksonville and the metropolitan community of Pulaski County, Arkansas. We moved, in fact, into the same apartment complex, and our apartment faced theirs. The sidewalk divided our apartments.

Of course, while I was stationed on military duty in Arkansas, your Father was born. He was a big baby at birth because he weighed over nine pounds. When his sister was born six years earlier, she weighed eight pounds, nine ounces. Yes! At birth, your Father was a big baby, but sadly, your fraternal Grandmother experienced some medical complications after your Father's birth. I believe she had an incompetent doctor who was concerned only about making more money. He induced Grandmom to have an earlier birth. Therefore, rather than wait for her to have a natural delivery, Grandmomma's doctor, I believe, performed an unnecessary cesarean section. Because of this surgical procedure, she experienced some serious medical complications.

Grand momma remained in the hospital for several more days. I took your Father home. Then, Grandma's parents took your Father and his sister to live with them briefly back in Memphis. But, as she remained hospitalized, Grand momma had another surgery called an ileostomy. About one week after being observed, she was discharged from the hospital. Her parents and I agreed meanwhile that it was best that Grandmom, your Father, and his sister moved temporarily with them to Memphis. They could better care for them than I could. After all, I was still on military duty, which required me to be present for duty.

Nonetheless, I thought that the medical procedures that Grand Momma's doctor performed on her were unnecessary. He performed an unnecessary procedure to induce her to give birth. In my estimation, the performance of this procedure bordered on medical malpractice. I began to discuss subsequently with grand momma and other family members the possibility of filing medical malpractice charges against her doctor.

So, to file malpractice charges, I made an appointment to speak with a group of lawyers in Jonesboro, Arkansas. Indeed, the process would be expensive and time-consuming. But, due in part to her youth and being back home in Memphis surrounded by close family members and dear friends, Grandmother was able to bounce back and regain her physical and mental health.

Assistance from Arkansas Attorney General Bill Clinton

grand momma was pregnant with your Father. Several months before his birth, she went to a local department store and placed $9.98 in a layaway account; however, later, she decided she did not want the item and wanted a refund. She asked the merchant, but he refused her refund request. So, I went directly to the store owner dressed in my United States Air Force uniform. I thought that he would refund the amount in question. "Sir, I am here to request that you refund $9.98 to my wife. This is all that I want. Most of your customers are stationed here at the Little Rock Air Force Base, like me and my family." Again, the store owner refused to issue a refund. Therefore, I obtained an appointment to speak to the base commander and staff to appeal to the merchant on behalf of your grandma and me. I was informed, "Sergeant Clayton, I am sorry. There is nothing we can do. The store is not physically located on the grounds of Little Rock Air Force Base."

I was, however, determined somehow and in some way, based on moral principles and standards, to get Grand Momma a refund of $9.98. I knew that God would help. I heard the voice of God speak to me. "Look in the Yellow Pages telephone directory under consumer complaints." I saw that the Arkansas Attorney General's office was located in downtown Little Rock. I discovered that Bill Clinton (the future president of America) was the attorney general. I submitted a consumer complaint with a copy of Grand momma's receipt for $9.98. Several days later, I received a telephone call from the merchant who told me to go to the store and pick up Grand momma's refund. And, even today, if former president Bill Clinton or his wife, Hilary Rodman-Clinton, is standing and participating in a cause that I can agree with based on a moral principle, they have my unwavering support.

Returning Home to Memphis
with a Word of Caution

My time remaining on active duty was quickly concluding. grand momma and I had several decisions to make: (1) I could reenlist for another four years in the Air Force, (2) I could relocate back to Memphis with my family and become a member of the Air National Guard, (3) I could enter graduate school at the Memphis Theological Seminary to continue my using veterans' educational benefits, (4) I could return to work with my employer United Parcel Service in Memphis. To make these decisions, I had to consider where we would live and what schools would be available for your Father and his sister to attend.

I discussed my situation with your grandma's first cousin, Michael. I explained the options that my wife, our children, and I were considering—staying in Jacksonville or moving back to Memphis. He responded, "Otis, I know my kinfolk. I know Aunt Ollie, her husband, sisters, and brothers. If you move your family back to Memphis, they will get into your business, and this will destroy your marriage to your wife. I know what I am talking about. Joyce and I and our children are not moving back to Memphis. Why? I do know Momma, my sisters, and my brothers. If we moved back to Memphis, they would do their level best to get into our marriage to destroy it. So, the best thing we can do is stay here in Arkansas. Otis, you are a grown man. I know that you are going to make up your mind. But, knowing what I know, if I were you, I would keep my family right here in Arkansas on this side of the Mississippi River."

A Marriage Relationship with a Sea of Disagreements

Long before your fraternal grand momma and I agreed to get married, I reminded her repeatedly that I wanted to marry her and legitimize our daughter through marriage. I did not want my daughter to be raised by another man. It is my conviction and belief that a mature and responsible man takes care of his children. If a man lies with a woman to make a baby, he must care for and provide for that baby.

Moreover, since I could not secure employment after graduating from LeMoyne Owen College, I informed her that I also desired to volunteer for service in the United States Air Force and obtain the veterans' educational benefits to pursue post-graduate studies. Obtaining a quality education is something that has been ingrained in my mind since I was a small child. "You can become anything you wish with a good education. This is something no White person or any other person can take from you." I have said the same thing to my children and anyone I have met.

grand momma and I have had the value of dissent education, and I wanted a secondary and college education for our children. Our children needed to attend historically Black institutions like Booker T. Washington High School, Hamilton High School, and LeMoyne Owen College.

Many family members and friends had attended and graduated from these institutions. Additionally, the teachers and administrators at these institutions, more likely than not, had gone to school with our parents and other family members and were members of the same religious and social organizations. My daughter and my wife came up with the strange idea that earning a high school diploma and a college education was more valuable, prestigious, and significant when the degree came from a White educational institution as opposed to a predominantly Black educational institution. Consequently, rather than attend local, predominantly Black institutions, your aunt graduated from Central High School and Memphis State University, now called the University of Memphis.

I came home for the weekend. At the time, I was attending post-graduate school at Vanderbilt University, 225 miles up the highway in Nashville. I was driving my car, and your Father was seated in the passenger seat. It was early Sunday morning, and we were going to Central Baptist Church. Reverend Dr. Reuben Green, my pastor, was out of town, and he had asked that I deliver the sermon. At the time, I knew that my son and your mother were dating. Within a few months, they would graduate from Hamilton High School, and they both had been accepted to begin the fall term at LeMoyne Owen College. I was excited for them. Their futures were as bright as the morning sun. Your Father said, "Daddy, can I tell you something?"

I said, "Yes. You can always tell me anything." Well, I want you to know that my girlfriend has missed her period."

I was in shock. I had so many high and noble expectations for your Father. I wanted him to have an enjoyable and relaxing college experience, something I had not had. He could focus on achieving academic excellence at LeMoyne Owen College and graduate school. But, when he told me that your Mother had missed her period, my dreams were shattered. I asked your Father, "Does her parents know this? He said, "Yes. They know." "Okay," I told him. "After church service, I will call them".

I preached the sermon to the waiting and attentive congregation at Central Baptist Church. But, at our first opportunity, your Father and I left. I called and spoke directly to your Mother's parents when we arrived home. I said, "My son informed me that your daughter missed her period. Did you know that?" They responded in the affirmative. We know, Mr. Clayton. I said, "I think that the most appropriate, responsive, and mature thing to do is for Otis Jr. to marry Natashia. But please allow me to talk with my wife about this. I will get back to you all later.

I talked to your fraternal grand momma about your Father and your Mother. Otis Jr. I said to her _____ "I think we need to sell this house and get a bigger house. Our son, _____, and his girlfriend will graduate from Hamilton High School. They can get married. His girlfriend can have our grandbaby. They can attend LeMoyne Owen College, and we can help them raise our grandchild.

However, your grand momma, _____strongly and vehemently rejected my suggestion. She argued, "Your Father was too young to get married. He is just seventeen years of age. "I disagreed, pointing out, "If our son is old enough to make a baby, he is old enough to care for his baby. This is the right time for him to grow up and become a mature young man."

Our different understanding about obtaining an education at historically Black institutions and Otis Jr. becoming responsible for his actions are one of many reasons why grand momma and I would ultimately separate and divorce. We began increasingly to have vastly different perspectives about life and living. Bad company ruins good morals.

A Revolutionary Preacher: A Member of a Long History of Preachers in our Families

I accepted, confessed, and believed in Jesus Christ at ten. My confession of faith was made at an annual revival meeting at the New Nonconnah Missionary Baptist Church, which took place after Vacation Bible School. The Pastor, Reverend Robert Lee Jones, the school bus driver, would pick up children and adults throughout the Geeter Subdivision of Whitehaven and transport them to church.

The Vacation Bible School classes were divided age-appropriate, but one of the goals was to eventually identify and locate individuals who were not Christian. So, after class for two weeks, we gathered in the church fellowship hall to enjoy lunch. After lunch, we gathered in the church sanctuary for the noon revival service. Pastor Jones invited one of his local Baptist church pastor friends to serve as the evangelist. Before the service, those students in the Bible class who were not believers were invited to take a seat on the mourner's bench. The evangelist, who typically was male, preached a powerful, passionate, and moving sermon. He would always conclude his sermon in a highly emotional manner and sang gospel songs such as "Amazing

Grace" or "Precious Lord." He opened the church's doors by asking those on the mourner's bench or the congregation, "Have you accepted Christ as your savior?" At one of these afternoon revival meetings, I became a follower of Christ.

Later that summer, I went to church on many different occasions with Aunt Willie Mae and her children, my first cousins. One night, I went with evangelist Wille Mae and my cousin to a Holiness Pentecostal revival in our community. It was held outside in a big tent. The preacher, Elder Lusk, was the pastor of my Aunt Willie Mae and some of my other relatives. Elder Lusk asked all the boys to call to the altar at the time of prayer. He said, "I want to pray and lay hands on you boys because God had revealed to me that one of you boys has been called to preach the gospel of Jesus Christ." (I thought was strange that no girls were asked to be involved.) He prayed for five to ten minutes and laid his hands on our heads. After his prayer, I believed God had called me to become a preacher. Still, I was afraid to say so because I strangely and mysteriously wanted someone to explain my call rationally and reasonably.

But unfortunately, I did not know any preacher who could explain the call to me. At that time, most preachers I knew, including Elder Lusk and my own Pastor Jones, had more religion in their hands and feet than they did within their heads. I was a Christian seeking and looking for a head-and-heart kind of religious experience. Like Saint Anslem, I wanted to believe so that I might understand.

Years later, after I graduated from LeMoyne Owen College, married, and volunteered for service in the United States Air Force, I finally learned what the call to the ministry entailed. I met an Air Force chaplain at the Seymour

Johnson Air Force Base in Goldsboro, North Carolina. He was the first African-American chaplain I had met who was a member of the clergy within the Baptist tradition. He was a married graduate of the Howard University School of Divinity. He was short in stature standing approximately five foot five. Strangely, I do not remember his name. Still, this chaplain was a highly talented and extremely powerful Baptist preacher who was a triple threat because he could preach, pray, and sing, as well as play the piano and organ. We worked together as members of the Seymour Johnson honor team, providing funeral services for deceased active and former military members.

After I met this chaplain, I used every opportunity to be in his presence. I finally got to ask him to explain the call to the ministry. Essentially, he said that the call to the ministry of Jesus Christ means that, as a Baptist minister, I must promise to dedicate my life to serving God and the people of God by going to school to educate and train myself for leadership. And, if I wanted to become a military chaplain, I must not only graduate from college, which I had, but I also must complete a four-year seminary education and meet physical requirements for joining the United States armed forces. Several years later, when I completed my active duty service, I was admitted and accepted as a graduate student at the Memphis Theological Seminary (MTS). Studying at MTS was a challenging experience because also worked at night for United Parcel Service and remained connected with the military as a Tennessee Air Force National Guard member.

Now, I am not the only preacher in my family. Reverend Columbus Clayton (Uncle Budda), and my brother,

Reverend Rickey Clayton, are clergy members. Uncle Bubba began preaching at fifteen as a boy preacher at the Lake Grove Missionary Baptist Church in Memphis. He was also a member of the Lake Grove Church Choir. Therefore, he can be described as a singing preacher. I can recall that when he concluded his sermon, Uncle Budda would sing "God would make a way somehow," and the congregation would always become caught emotionally in the spirit. There was an atmosphere of singing and shouting for joy.

When Uncle Bubba graduated from Geeter High School, he relocated to Saginaw, Michigan, and began to work for the General Motors Corporation, but he also was a bi-vocational preacher. While employed for General Motors, he was also called to serve as the pastor of the New Jerusalem Missionary Baptist Church.

Unlike Uncle Bubba and me, my brother Rickey has never served as a congregation pastor. He is one of the associate ministers at the New Nonconnah Missionary Baptist Church. In that capacity, he helps teach Sunday school classes, occasional preaches, and volunteers to serve whatever need arises.

I know there are preachers on your mother's side of the family. Sell Jackson was both your mother's and your maternal Grandmother's Father. Further, as I understand, Sell Jackson served as a loving husband and bi-vocational clergy working at the Firestone Rubber Company and then served at the Alpha Church in West Memphis, Arkansas.

I remember Pastor Sell Jackson during my student days with Aunt Ruby. Pastor Jackson would occasionally drop by to visit Ruby in our classroom at Geeter Elementary School. I particularly enjoyed his visits to our classroom because he would always bring treats for the teacher and students of Aunt Ruby. Pastor Sell Jackson was additionally the son and grandson of ministers. Oh, yes! The bloodline and mindset of being and serving as a minister is a flooding river within your family history. Does this mean that you are also to become a minister? That is a decision between you and God Almighty.

Honestly, I do not know, but God knows. The God whom I have come to know and believe in through my own personal experience does not serve as a dictator, and neither are you a robot. God allows us to have free will to make our own decisions regarding how we are live our lives. I continue to insist nonetheless that anyone who makes the decision to accept the call to the ministry is challenged always to do his or her best to become the best-prepared minister possible.

As a preacher, I remain an active member of various socially and politically engaged organizations. I am just being truthful and faithful to my calling and what our ancestors in the African American religious experience have given me. I have worked endlessly to develop a variable ministry with an action plan that addresses the longings, desires, and aspirations of God's people.

Chapter 4

MY LETTER TO MY SON: BECOME POLITICALLY ENGAGED

My First Sermon on Your Birthday:
A Defining Moment

I came off active duty from Little Rock Air Force Base at Jacksonville, Arkansas, a few months before your first birthday. If you do not know it, you were born at the Doctor's Hospital in Little Rock, Arkansas. For the first few months in Memphis, you, your sister, your mother, and I lived with your maternal grandparents, PaP Joe, Grandmom Ollie. Your mother and I were married four years earlier before you were born. A few days later, I enlisted in the United States Air Force. I left your mother and your sister in Memphis. I went to boot camp for six weeks in San Antonio, Texas, where I learned how to become a soldier. This involved doing everything the military way—physical fitness, wearing the military uniform, marching in military formation, standing at attention, learning military courteousness, breaking down and remaking military weapons, and learning about teamwork.

After graduating from boot camp, I received military orders; I was assigned to Seymour Johnson Air Force Base in Goldsboro, North Carolina. I flew from San Antonio back to Memphis. I stayed there with your mother and Felecia for a few days. Then, I drove eight hundred miles to Seymour Johnson. I reported to my duty station and met my squadron commander and supervisor, who explained my duties and responsibilities to me. My supervisor assigned a fellow soldier and coworker to help me secure off-base housing.

The most efficient and cost-effective housing that I found was a house trailer. Then, a few weeks later, I drove back to Memphis to get your mother and Felecia. At that time, we loaded up my car and then kissed, hugged, and said good-bye to your mother's family and my family. We made it back to Goldsboro, North Carolina, and lived there for two years.

While I was stationed there at Seymour Johnson Air force base, I met my first Black chaplain. Like me, he was a distinguished graduate of the Howard University School of Divinity and a member of the Baptist Church. We were members of the Seymour Johnson Honor Guard Detail. When an active-duty member or veteran died, we worked as a team to conduct military honors for the family. However, during our relationship, this chaplain explained what it means to be called to the ministry and what I must do to become a chaplain. Of course, he stated simply that the call means that I must accept the commitment to serve

God and God's people and work tirelessly to prepare myself academically for spiritual leadership. Further, to become a chaplain, I need to be physically fit, become a member of the clergy, complete the seminary education, obtain an ecclesiastical endorsement from my denomination, and apply to become a chaplain in the military.

When we returned home to Memphis, I followed that chaplain's advice. I applied, was accepted at the Memphis Theological Seminary, and became a minister at the Mount Moriah East Baptist Church. Reverend _____ allowed me to preach my first sermon. I preached the sermon from the Book of Habakkuk, chapter 2. I entitled my sermon "Destroyed for Lack of Knowledge." But in a real sense, I believed that sermon text was somehow an abiding reflection of the story my grandfather, Silas Clayton Sr. (PaPa), who had told me about his grandfather, Aaron Clayton. Aaron had been an American slave who desperately wanted his freedom. He obtained his freedom when President Abraham Lincoln signed the Emancipation Proclamation. This proclamation enabled Aaron and other emancipated slaves to obtain the knowledge that they, their children, grandchildren, and future generations needed to live a better quality of life. Now, surprisingly, I preached this sermon about knowledge on your second birthday. I know that knowledge is also something you will need in the days ahead.

Football and Controversy

You were a big baby at birth, weighing nine pounds. You never missed a meal. Subsequently, you were bigger than most children your age. I learned there was a Little League football program in nearby Whitehaven.

When we moved back to Memphis, we secured an apartment out east in the Raleigh-Bartlett community. Your mother worked as the apartment complex manager, which allowed us to live for free in an apartment on the property, but we had to pay a monthly utility bill. Meanwhile, a house came available for sale at 1785 Wendy Drive next door to your grandparents, Momma Ollie and PaPa Joe. I told your mother, "_____I can use my veteran's benefits to purchase that house. We do not know when your employer may terminate you without warning."

"But, Otis," she replied, "I don't want us to move there. It's too close to Momma and Daddy. It may cause problems for us." I continued, "_____, we can also rent out the house. Or we can let my Uncle Rickey live there. Rickey is single. He lives with my mother. You don't know when your employer may fire you and tell us we have only a few days to move out." Eventually, your mother agreed with the logic of my position. We purchased our first home while still residing on your mother's company property. Uncle Rickey moved in and secured our home. Now, low and behold, several months later, my prediction became a reality. Your mother's employer decided to terminate her. We had two weeks to move off company property.

I immediately informed Uncle Rickey of our unfortunate circumstances. He moved back with my mother. We moved quickly into our home at 1785 Wendy Drive. It was less than five miles north of Whitehaven, where I got you involved in Little League football. You played football for Coach John for the Dallas Cowboys.

I got you involved with football because it would help you develop socialization, leadership skills, and responsibilities as you mixed with boys your age. Playing Little League football afforded you, at an early age, an excellent opportunity to flourish.

Your mother disagreed vehemently, however, with you being involved in football. You were, after all, big for your age, but you were only four. She kept saying, "Otis Jr. is my baby, and I am afraid that he will eventually get hurt playing football." Indeed, your mother is a sweet, kind, and loving mother; otherwise, she would not be the mother of my children and grandmother of my grandchildren. We all have our shortcomings. I may be more military-oriented than I ought to be. Meanwhile, your beloved mother suffered from a form of complacency. She refused to take some time to look into the mirror at herself and say, "How can I develop my own level of intelligence?" And, then she could do something about that.

A Child Who Will Never Be

I wanted to have at least four children in my marriage to your mother. I advised your mother on many occasions about my desire for more children. After your sister's birth, your mother and I took the necessary precautions to prevent her from becoming pregnant. While I used condoms, your mother also took the birth control pill. However, when we got married, your mother and I agreed to try to have at least one and maybe two children. I wanted to have at least one son. I wanted to have a son named Otis Clayton Jr. Well! Our dreams became true when she became pregnant with you. You were born a healthy, bouncing baby. We were both delighted and overjoyed.

When we moved from Little Rock to Memphis, your mother and I were surprised to learn that she was pregnant. I do not believe she was more than one to two months along. She had missed no more than two periods. But your mother advised me that she was not interested in having any more children. I disagreed with her. I wanted one or two more children. However, I was not a misogynist, and I made it a point to listen carefully to my wife and be attentive to her. After all, I would not be the one to carry a baby for nine months. I went along with your mother to have this pregnancy terminated. You had a sibling who will never be. The abortion issue was a button issue over forty years ago. The abortion issue remains an explosive issue today. However, the mental health of the mother is of primary importance.

Being Involved with My Children's Education

You and your sister _____had an excellent educational foundation. When your mother was pregnant with you, I read and talked to her stomach. I just believed that you could hear me in some mysterious way even as she carried you to term. When you were born, I continued to read and talk to you. Your mother and I agreed to enroll both of you in Montessori schools. This continued for several years. When both of you began elementary school, we intentionally enrolled you in the parochial school system at Saint Augustine. We planned that you would attend from the first through sixth grades. We believed that the classroom size was smaller there than in it was I the public school system. The small size allowed you to enjoy more personal attention from your teachers to strengthen you in all subject areas.

When you and your sister began to attend public schools, I saw immediately how the Montessori and parochial school systems had given you an upper hand compared to students who had spent their educational experience solely in public schools. I saw evidence of my assertion when I began substituting teaching in the Memphis school system. I made it a point to volunteer as a substitute teacher at the school you and Felecia attended. If you recall, when you were a student, I substitute taught at Alcy Road Elementary School, Corry Junior High School, and Hamilton High School.

I became the president of the Alcy Road School Parent and Teachers Organization. This afforded me the unique opportunity to go behind the scenes and learn about the local school system's inner workings and establish enduring friendships and relationships. In short, I obtained a bird' birds-eye view of what it takes to become an effective teacher and how staff members were hired at Alcy Road School. Further, I worked closely with Mrs. Johnson, the principal at Alcy Road School. Her entire family, for the most part, was employed in the Memphis public school system. While Carl Johnson Sr. was a Memphis school board member, her son, _____ served as principal at Westwood High School. Because of my association with Alcy Road Schools, Principal _____recruited and hired me to become a secondary educator at his school.

Butting Heads with Me

I indeed applauded and was excited that you had graduated from Hamilton High School. It was from that school that your devoted mother, her siblings, and several of my younger siblings had graduated. As a substitute teacher at Hamilton High School, I enjoyed a cordial and friendly relationship with the principal, assistant principal, teachers, and other staff members. You had also applied to and were accepted to begin your undergraduate studies at my alma mater, LeMoyne Owen College. However, in all honesty, I had some troubling concerns about you. They included your girlfriend _____pregnancy and how to deal with it, and your burning desire to become a member of the Omega Phi Psi Fraternity.

Your girlfriend_____parents agreed with me that, ideally, the most mature and responsible thing to do was that you and Natashia should marry. I explained to her parents that my wife and I would purchase a bigger house in Whitehaven or Twinkle Town. You and your girlfriend _____ would move in. We could help take care of our grandchild-to-be. You and your girlfriend could continue your education at LeMoyne Owen College.

However, your mother was incensed and highly disturbed by any discussion about you marrying Natashia. Her primary rejoinder was, "Otis Jr is definitely too young to get married." My reply in part was, "I had known his girlfriend _____mother's family before she was born. I attended Geeter Elementary School with her mother, Aunt Ruby, and her other siblings. They were devoted and devout Christians. Our son's girlfriend_____ grandfather and great-grandfather were all preachers. Furthermore, her family members are all hard-working people. I would be thrilled and thankful to God that Natashia would become my daughter-in-law."

Eleven months later, your girlfriend ____ had two young children, ____ (Threi) and his sister ____. Again and again, your mother and I had heated discussions about what was best for you and, most importantly, for both you and your children. Threi and his sister ____ were helpless infants who needed loving parents and a secure and comfortable home environment. Long term, you need to accept responsibility and know you must put away childish things and become a man. If you did not make a responsible and mature decision, you would begin to have the attitude that everyone and the world owed you something.

I even suggested to your mother that, although you were a college student, you could become a member of the Air National Guard. It would enable you to obtain financial support for college and income to support your children. However, instead of wanting the best for maturity and responsibility, your mother did her best to shelter and prevent you from accepting your moral obligations and actions. She suggested that everybody does not need to go into the military. In some respect, I do agree with her. But I suggested the Air National Guard service as a way of helping you, your children, and your future. Your mother had no interest in that. She refused to cut the umbilical cord by allowing you to accept responsibility. You were still her little boy baby.

Before beginning your studies at LeMoyne Owen College, I strongly advise you that your primary focus must first be your academic studies. You really did not have any time to pledge to a fraternity. You needed to wait until your junior year before you considered pleading with any fraternity. Rather, on the other hand, in addition to your studies, you must work a job to help Natashia financially with your son, Otis III. I recall that you began to work at a restaurant in East Memphis. You completed the first semester and made the dean's list. This was a joyous moment.

Suddenly, you began to come home later and later. I asked, "You son _____, are you working anywhere?" "Daddy. No. I am not working." "But, Son, you know my policy. If you are not working and come home after midnight without calling me or your mother to inform us, you will have a problem with me." Then, without calling, you continued to come home after midnight. I asked you again, "Otis, what is the problem? You refused to call to let me or your mother that you will arrive at midnight." Finally, you said, "Daddy, I am online. I am pledging Omega Psi Phi." This did not make me happy., I strongly urge you not to consider fraternity membership until your junior year. Yet, you had defied my recommendation. However, since you were eighteen years of age, you no longer needed my consent. You were, for all practical purposes, considered a grown man.

You were still living in the Otis Clayton Sr. and _____household, and we had established rules and guidelines for you to follow. You kept butting heads with me. You had graduated from high school and were now in college. This was a momentous achievement. Most African American men your age were either unemployed, incarcerated, or high school dropouts. Many were leaving our women with children to raise. However, with the irrational support of your mother, you developed an iconoclastic attitude. When I was your age, I went to school full-time and worked full-time. My mother and siblings depended on me to support them to some degree. You had it made in the shade and did not know it.

Since you were unwilling to follow our rules and guidelines, I counseled you repeatedly that you needed to find another place to live. For me, this counsel was a bitter pill to swallow, and it created increased disagreement and dissatisfaction among me, your mother, and other family members.

A Promising and Troubling Association

I became aware of Professor and Pastor Reuben Green and his wife, Mildred Green, also a professor, during my matriculation at LeMoyne Owen College. While Professor Green taught music, Professor Reuben Green served as chaplain and taught classes in philosophy and religion. I intentionally avoided taking any classes dealing with religion. I was running from my calling to the ministry; I wanted nothing to do with preachers or religion. But Reverend David Boyle was a young preacher whom I did meet one day while walking across the college campus. He did not advise me that he was a member of the clergy. However, he expressed his ambition to attend Bishop College in Dallas, Texas.

Years went by quickly. Finally, I completed my active-duty service in the United States Air Force, and we returned to Memphis. I worked at night for United Parcel Service, was a member of the Air National Guard, and had become a graduate school at the Memphis Theological Seminary (MTS). My income and your mother's enabled us to live a comfortable lifestyle.

Deacon Ernest Washington and his wife, Sarah, lived across the street from PaPa Joe and Momma Olive. They were the best of friends to us and were instrumental in helping to raise your mother and her siblings. When we returned to Memphis, your mother and I asked Deacon Washington and his wife about Mount Moriah East Missionary Baptist Church (MMEMBC) and its pastor, _____. Based on their recommendation, we later discussed the possibility of becoming members of MMEMBC. Finally, we became members there. I was later licensed to preach by Pastor Smith and the board of deacons at MMEMBC.

I was seated in the Memphis Theological Seminary library and was involved in my reading, research, and writing. Reverend Harold Chandler, an assistant MTS librarian, referred an African-American female reporter from the Memphis *Commercial Appeal* newspaper to interview me. She was writing a story about Black churches in Memphis. I provided her with my comments, which later appeared in the newspaper.

Pastor _____was my minister, and we also had several things in common. We were both graduates of Booker T. Washington High School and LeMoyne College. We were also products of living and striving in the ghetto streets of South Memphis. But, unlike me, he was not a graduate of a seminary rather than a graduate school. Pastor _____ called my home and requested that I go to his office for a talk. When we met, he said, "So many pastors and preachers throughout Memphis are angry with you. You made comments that they strongly disagreed with. You need to be careful about what you say to newspaper reporters. They take what you say and then write something different." Although I was a member of MMEMBC, I was not a paid staff member.

Additionally, previously, I had received notes from Pastor _____ that I believed were increasingly intellectually annoying. One stated, "Otis, I do not want you or any other minister here to enter the pulpit unless I invite you." Another reminded me, "Before you are ordained as a minister of MMEMBC, you must carry some bags for other pastors and preachers."

I began to take stock of my relationship and association with Pastor _____. I had become uncomfortable with his leadership style and his preparation for ministry. Could I not, in good conscience, continue to follow his example as my spiritual leader? So, I began having quiet talks and discussions with fellow seminary students. One was David Boyle. I told David, "I have the ambition to become a pastor and a chaplain. After graduation from MTS, I'm interested in ordination and becoming a military chaplain in the Air National Guard. But I am interested in being mentored by a pastor who has at least a seminary education. I want my pastor to have been where I am trying to go." After our conversation, David suggested that I contact Reverend Doctor Reuben Green.

Reverend Green was a native of Oklahoma. He graduated at sixteen from high school and Bishop College in Dallas, Texas, Oberlin Theological Seminary, and Vanderbilt University School of Divinity. Additionally, he was a member of many social organizations. During his student days at Oberlin, he met and married Mildred Davis-Green, who later obtained her post-graduate degree in music. They both were known locally, statewide, and nationally because of their work in the National Baptist Church Convention, USA, Incorporated, and LeMoyne Owen College.

Indeed, Reverend Green was a perfect fit for me; he was the kind of pastor I had been seeking who could help and mentor me. I felt confident that he would not be intimidated by my educational ministry preparation. So, after we met and talked about my intentions, I became a Central Baptist Church, Incorporated member. Shortly after I graduated from MTS, Pastor Green ordained me at the church in an ordination service. Reverend Boyle preached my ordination sermon.

I preached at several self-supporting congregations in Memphis. I was not considered a permanent pastor for any one of them. Still, I was called to become the pastor of the Antioch Missionary Baptist Church (ABC) in Batesville, Mississippi, about sixty miles south of Memphis. For a while, everything went well. The congregation was growing both numerally and financially. ABC was raising more money weekly than it had ever in its history. And it was also raising more than my home church, Central Baptist Church.

Then, trouble came to the church that I was unable to handle. The deacon surprised me with two bits of information: (1) the congregation had the right to elect the pastor annually, and (2) I would not be compensated for the increased income being raised by the congregation. I replied,

"Can you show me that in the Bible?" They could not do that because there was no such animal in the Bible.

Since I had never pastored a congregation before, I sought counsel from two other pastors, Pastor Reuben Green, and Pastor De Wayne Hill. Pastor Green advised, "Otis, if I were you, I would simply resign. You can always get another church somewhere else." I told Pastor Hill what Pastor Green had advised. Pastor Hill remarked, "Otis, do not listen to what Pastor Green said. Green is like so many preachers. He is jealous of you because he knows you have a good church. You are raising more money at your church than he is raising at Central. He has a church in the city of Memphis. You have a church in the country, yet since you have been at Antioch, you are teaching your congregation how to give. You are raising more money every week than Green is."

Sadly, I walked away from the church sometime after that without resigning. I began to work for FedEx and reconnected with the Air National Guard. However, I could not identify and secure a vacant Baptist church congregation in Memphis.

Getting Involved in What Is Going On Politically

I relocated later to Denver, Colorado, for an opportunity to work with the Department of Veterans Affairs. I did not know anyone there. You are aware of the clandestine and surreptitious manner in which I had been blackballed and those people who were involved. Again, I remember that Pastor Alfred Hill told me he thought my pastor was jealous of me. Pastor Greene was also a ringleader with a group of Black pastors in Memphis. They allowed only certain ministers to secure Black Baptist congregations throughout the metropolitan community of Memphis. It had nothing to do with me being a highly trained minister. I possess five degrees from prestigious institutions of higher learning, such as Vanderbilt University. But Pastor Green and those preachers did not care about my preparation for ministry. I was not part of their clique.

Nonetheless, when I relocated to Denver, I did know there were fellow veterans, members of the Omega Psi Phi Fraternity Incorporated, and members of the clergy who were residents there. Pastor Green had mentioned previously that he had taken a sabbatical leave from Central Baptist Church and LeMoyne College to study at Iliff Theological Seminary in Denver. During that study period, he fellowshipped with Senior Pastor Williams and New Hope Baptist Church members.

So, because of this blackball dilemma in Memphis, God blessed me with employment with the Health Care Administration Division of the Department of Veterans Affairs in Denver. I moved to Denver for employment and never looked back. I called the New Hope Baptist Church, and the church secretary introduced me to Deacon _____ who drove me around and showed me my work location. In short, Deacon _____, his wife, and their wonderful family extended kindness and generosity. Also, on my arrival in Denver, I reached out to a member of the Denver Chapter of Omega Psi Phi Fraternity, but I was initially unable to receive any assistance.

I will, throughout eternity, give thanks and praise to God that I am a veteran of the US military. I researched and discovered, to my amazement, that Reverend Taylor, the senior pastor at the United Methodist Church, was a retired chaplain; he served in the United States Air Force. I called him and identified myself as Reverend Doctor Otis Clayton Sr., United States Army (retired) chaplain and expressed interest in locating and identifying lodging. He said, "Chaplain Clayton, I am honored to hear from you. Please give me a few days to call around my friends at the Retired Enlisted Association." Roughly two days later, Reverend Taylor called me. "Chaplain Clayton, I think I may have a veteran and his family for you to lodge with. Can you make it to my office tomorrow evening at seven? I'd like you to meet a veteran named Charles Wong."

I said to myself, *I think Charles Wong is an Asian brother.* Honestly, I did not care what nationality, race, color, or religion he was. He and his family offered me to live with them temporarily. To my astonishment and surprise, when I saw and met Charles Wong, I saw that he was an African American, and I learned that he was from Louisiana. His fraternal grandfather had relocated to America from China to work on building the railroad system, and he had met Charles's grandmother in America. His grandparents had several children, one of which was his father. Then, Charles's father and mother had twelve children. When he graduated from high school, Charles enlisted in the Air Force and served through the aftermath of the Korean and Vietnam Wars. He spent over twenty years wearing the uniform, retired at Lowry Air Force Base in Denver, and worked another twenty-plus year for the United States Post Office.

I will never forget Charles will always be a dear friend and brother. He took me around and introduced me to various churches and to one veteran's organization called The Retired Enlisted Association (TREA), Chapter 3, in Aurora. The city of Aurora is essentially right across the street from Denver and is more than twice the geographic size of Denver. Previously, because of taxes and other reasons, former residents of Denver broke off and established the city of Aurora.

Charles took me around to places like his Church of Christ, which was a Congregational fellowship. I enjoyed the hospitality and fellowship of his congregation, but I was more at home with other congregations and with my fellow comrades at TREA. The Denver TREA was made up of approximately 1500 members, which made it the largest chapter that was predominantly Black in the United States. Shortly after that, I joined TREA and was elected chaplain for the chapter. As a chaplain, I quickly became the most powerful and influential voice in Chapter 3 and within the metropolitan community of Aurora/Denver. Also, as chaplain, I became essentially the organization's unofficial pastor and spiritual leader. Although I was not a paid staff person, I opened and closed meetings with prayer, married members, gave eulogies for members and their family members, visited sick members at home and in hospitals, and guests to speak to the TREA Chapter 3 membership on special occasions.

I invited the Reverend Dr. _____ to speak at our TREA Black History Program one year. Though not a veteran, he was the senior pastor at the Brenan Baptist Church in Memphis, Tennessee. He and I had been friends for years because we met during our graduate studies at Memphis Theological Seminary. We had both been instructors at the Tennessee School of Religion. This noncredited interdenominational school offered classes to people in the Old Testament, New Testament, homiletics, theology, etc. Further, Reverend _____and I were both alumnae of historically Black institutions like Booker T. Washington High School and Tennessee State University and were fellow members of the same fraternity, Omega Psi Phi Fraternity Incorporated.

My involvement in TREA created unique opportunities for me to participate and get involved with other social and political organizations like Leadership Aurora and the Colorado Leadership Circle. The training and connections I received through Leadership Aurora connected me with political leaders throughout Colorado. I established a close connection with the superintendent of Aurora Public Schools, John Barry. I advised him that I was a former public school secondary educator, and I had a son who was a Memphis and Shelby County administrator. Superintendent Barry told me to inform my son that countless administrative and leadership opportunities were available in Aurora, Colorado.

I actively participated in and supported Michael Hancock's election to become Denver County's mayor. Like the previous elections of Wellington Webb, Mayor Hancock's election revealed that the residents of Denver County, like most Colorado residents, are extremely progressive. For instance, while Denver County is no more than 10 percent African American, the voters of Denver County overwhelmingly voted for the mayor based on substance and not necessarily based on the color of the candidates' skin.

Through my involvement and leadership with TREA and Leadership Aurora, I volunteered and worked with Colorado Leadership Circle by connecting with Rosemary _____ the state coordinator for the office of United States Senator _____. Rosemary is one of the many Latin Americans in Colorado working continuously through endless political and social involvement. Rosemary and I met at one of the TREA chapter meetings, and I inquired about the effort in Colorado to reelect United States President Obama. In turn, my dear friend Rosemary referred me to James _____, the coordinator for Colorado Leadership.

Jim is a tall and handsome native Coloradoan who earned degrees in government from Harvard University and finance from Stanford University. Although he is now the chief executive officer for North American Specialty Hospital, he helped coordinate the 2008 Democratic Convention in Denver, was a candidate to become the superintendent of Denver Public Schools and was a commissioner for the Colorado Department of Education.

Jim and I became fast friends. He advised me that, although my participation was voluntary, I could obtain access to President Obama, but it came at a price. The Colorado Leadership Circle needed financial resources to host Obama and his representatives, who would travel to Colorado and visit occasionally. Admittedly, I did not pay the price of participation as Jim did. He is a multi-millionaire, but I did pay several thousand dollars for participation.

When Obama visited Colorado, I was blessed to be in the company of Michelle ____, the first lady, and Valerie _____, who served as President Obama's special advisor. I particularly enjoyed meeting Valerie. I used that meeting as an opportunity to flirt with her. The Colorado Leadership Circle hosted a meeting for Valerie at the home of Jim _____ girlfriend on Market Street in the heart of Denver. At the time, Jim's girlfriend was out of town attending a family member's funeral in Great Britain.

I parked my car on Market Street and walked cautiously to the residence. The security detail for Valerie Jared was substantial. I walked up to the residence and informed security who I was: "I am Dr. Otis Clayton, a member of the Colorado Leadership Circle." They checked the guest list and saw that my name was on it. The security detail frisked me and allowed me to enter.

When I entered the home, I saw a cross-section of people who were primarily White; there were no more than five African Americans. The total number of people present was no more than forty. Jim stood up front in the rather large, luxurious living room area. I saw Valerie Jared; she had entered the room as I entered. She was what I called a light, bright, and damn near gorgeous African American woman. With her body and physique, I could tell she was an amateur athlete and that she took excellent care of her mind, body, and soul. Valerie sat in a tall chair and looked at everyone in attendance. She wore a gorgeous light-colored blue dress. Jim introduced Valerie to us.

Jim asked us individually to say who we were and what we were doing in the campaign. I was the last person to introduce myself. But, before I could do anything, Jim said, "Valerie, I want you to meet my friend, the Reverend Dr. Otis Clayton. He is a retired United States Army chaplain. We thank him for his service to our great nation. He works in the campaign as a veterans' spokesman for the reelection of President Obama. Dr. Clayton, what do you have to say to Valerie?"

All eyes were on me. Everyone waited patiently for me to say something to Valerie Jared, the senior advisor to President Barack Obama. Before meeting Valerie, I had read her entire background and family history. Her father completed his medical training at Howard University. Her mother was a highly trained educator. Valerie was born in Syria, where her father and family had moved to work in their fields of endeavor. Valerie and her family subsequently moved back to America to live in Chicago. At an early age, Valerie completed boarding school in the northeast, completed her legal education at Harvard, got married, had one daughter, and later divorced.

So, since was single, I assumed Valerie _____ was also available. I gave my best shot of what I had to say: "Valerie, Hello! I am so honored and privileged to meet you in the flesh finally. You know, I have seen pictures of you on television, in magazines, and in newspapers. But please believe me—those pictures on television do not do you justice. You are even more beautiful in person." For the remainder of that meeting with the Colorado Leadership Circle—and I am not bragging or boasting—Valerie _____ kept her eyes on me. I know that I had said something that moved and touched her emotionally.

I did not, unfortunately, have an opportunity to further dialogue with Valerie _____. Before that meeting concluded, I departed to attend a scheduled meeting at TREA. If I had not departed, I wondered what would have happened regarding developing a friendship with the beautiful and intelligent senior advisor to President Obama.

Later that year, Jim and I traveled to Aspen, Colorado, to meet with the United States Senator, _____Harris. Our journey was on the heels of President Obama's reelection victory. Harris addressed a statewide meeting of democratic party official members, touching on a wide range of issues, the most important being democratic unity to support President Obama's agenda for the nation and the landscape of Colorado. At the time, Jim and I stood in line to meet and shake hands with the talented, intelligent, and gorgeous senator from California.

I have realized that I am simply a political animal—not that I will sell my soul to anyone. My ancestors, like Aaron Clayton and Silas Clayton Sr., did not sell out. If any of us is going to provide any meaningful and significant to help others, we must, as American citizens, become more politically astute. I have typically voted most of my life for democratic candidates. I do enjoy, however, soliciting productive dialogue with Americans who are Republicans and independents. I am confident that independents, Republicans, and Democrats can fight against economic inequality together to make America a better nation.

Chapter 5

MY LETTER TO ONE OF MY NIECES: LGBTQ SENSIBILITY

Keeping the Relationship between Your Father and Me at a Distance

I intentionally kept all the guys my Sister and your mother, _____dated at a distance. I had no personal vendetta against your father, Wallace (Bubba) Williams Jr.; instead, I operated with the mindset and the attitude that no man she dated was good enough for her. In other words, I served as the patriarch of our household. I worked full-time throughout high school and college to help Momma care for her household. I was the big brother who was also the protector and enforcer. My nickname in the streets of the South Memphis community was Crookethead; I was known as a no-nonsense, rough thug who did not tolerate anyone harassing, intimidating, or hitting any of his siblings or kinfolk.

After my daughter was born, I spent the summer with Granddaddy Aaron in Saginaw, Michigan. After completing my first year, I planned to drop out of LeMoyne Owen College. With the help of Granddaddy Aaron, I wanted to obtain a job working for his employer, General Motors Corporation (GMC). The company provided excellent wages, insurance, and other benefits for employees. My employment there would help provide for my daughter and her mother, _____GMC had a unique history as a union employer with the United Automotive Workers of hiring Blacks and people of color so they could have better lives. So, employment there would empower me ultimately to stand up to the plate to better provide for Felecia and Jackie. If I got that job, I would marry and relocate my family to Saginaw.

During that entire summer after completing my first year of college, I did various things to create income to give Aunt ____money so that she could take care of my daughter. After all, since we were not married, Aunt Jackie and Felecia lived with their parents. While I resided with Grandaddy Aaron, I worked temporarily in nearby Bay City, loading and unloading cargo ships, playing the numbers game, and hustling games of pool against my relatives and friends. However, the summer quickly ended, and I still had not secured a job with GMC.

In all honesty, Granddaddy Aaron did not want me to quit college. Unlike me, he understood from experience that the work at the Malleable Iron Foundry of GMC was extremely hard and strenuous. One of his fingers had been severed when he worked at the foundry. Although my father was not a high school graduate, he believed that the best plan for me and my daughter, in the long run, was for me to remain in college. Education is a short-term sacrifice for long-term gain. He echoed similar sentiments to those of his fraternal father, great-grandfather, and other ancestors. So, he resisted helping me without telling me specifically that he did not want to help me obtain employment at GMC. However, by his inaction, he revealed to me that graduating from college was best for me. I said, "Daddy, I know you can talk to your union representative, your supervisor, your Masonic brothers, my uncles, and other friends to help with employment."

I deeply resented that Granddaddy Aaron was unwilling to assist me in obtaining a manufacturing job with GMC. So, although the fall term at LeMoyne College had started, I caught a Greyhound bus reluctantly and traveled from Saginaw back home to Memphis. grand momma Elizabeth picked me up in her 1968 Blue Ford Comet four-door station wagon. She had purchased that kind of car because her family was growing. So, we drove home from the bus station to Chezita Garden.

When we arrived, I discovered, to my amazement, that my brother-in-law, _____, had committed an unpardonable sin. My brother, _____, enlisted in the United States Air Force and left home to boot camp training at Lackland Air Force Base in San Antonio, Texas. Without asking Edward's permission, Arthur had gone into our home, into Edward's closet, and begun to wear his clothes. Then I discovered that your mother and her husband _____had separated. Your Mother returned home because her husband had become angry and hit her. I became irritated, and I blew my stack. It was time for me to teach him a lesson. When I found him, he sat in the neighborhood barbershop, getting his hair cut. I jumped on him and began to beat him without any mercy. We were escorted out of the barbershop, and the police were called on me for disturbing the peace.

He and I later appeared before a Memphis judge, and I was absolved from all charges. I came to realize from that experience that, in a real sense, African-American men do not usually have any problems with the criminal justice system when they fight or injure one another. But, on the other hand, when an African American man has an altercation with a White man, the criminal justice system will place the total weight of the law on him. In addition, I came to understand that I needed to, at best, try to avoid coming between couples who were experiencing marital difficulties. Although I came to your mother's defense, she and her husband reconciled their differences and got back together. But my relationship with him was never the same. He began to tiptoe around me anytime we were in each other's presence.

Raising a Son to Amend His Grandfather's Shortcomings

Your beloved father, _____, and I were never close friends. It was not his problem; it had more to do with me than with him. Again, I had a mindset that did not allow us to become close friends. After all, he was dating my Sister. But Bubba and my brother, _____were much more congenial with one another. They hung around together and spent time going places together. This could be one of the reasons that Bubba began to date my Sister.

Although they were unrelated, Bubba was also best friends with my brother-in-law, one of my ex-wife's brothers. _____and Bubba had grown up together within the Alcy Road community. They lived down the street from one another. Their parents were close friends who also had roughly the same number of children of similar ages. Like me, Bubba and _____ were the same age and had attended the same schools from elementary school, junior high school to high school. Then, when _____dropped out of high school to enlist in the United States Navy, Bubba did likewise. However, _____remained in the Navy and retired after serving our great nation for over twenty years. However, unlike_____ , Bubba experienced tremendous difficulty in adjusting to Navy life. He could not spend the six months required to be classified as a veteran. Bubba received a dishonorable discharge that stigmatized him for gainful employment for the remainder of his days. He could not obtain federal, state, county, or city government employment. Your father, Bubba, had a taint on his reputation for the rest of his life.

You had four children: ___, I never had conversations with all of your children regarding military service. But I had several conversations with one of your son regarding a career, and he expressed interest in working with computers. "Uncle Otis," he said, "I enjoy working with computers and want to attend a technical school to obtain training and certification in computers."

"_____" I replied, "it will cost a ton of money to go technical school or college to obtain computer training. Also, have you ever traveled within America and to other countries?" "No," said Uncle Otis. "I don't have any money for computer training at technical school or college. I have never traveled to any other states in America or other countries, but I would love to travel someday."

I advised him to consider military service, explicitly taking the Air Force qualifying exam to be considered as a volunteer for service in the Air Force working with computers. During several conversations, I further advised him how his uncles and I had served in the Army and the Air Force. I thought that adding that, in some small manner, if your son would make the decision to join the Air Force, he somehow could rescue the tarnished military reputation of his grandfather. .

Now, I did teach one of your other sons. He had been one of my students at Sherwood Junior High School. I would sometimes drop him off at home if he needed a ride. Like other students, he would see me when I wore my United States Army uniform to school. I talked to him as I would all my students about what I did in the Army National Guard. I was a chaplain and was responsible for providing spiritual and religious support to the soldiers and their family members of my military battalion.

However, I do not recall having a specific conversation about him enlisting in the military. Your son may have talked about military service with one of my brothers or another family member. He took the Air Force qualifying exam in high school and earned an acceptable score. Then, after graduation, your son volunteered to enlist in the Air Force. He went to boot camp at Lackland Air Force Base and was later assigned to an Air Force Base in Alaska.

No Apology for Being Who You Are:
God Is Concerned About All People

I have had the privilege to travel to various places in our world. Most recently, I traveled to Medellin, Colombia in South America. I was invited to visit Medellin for several years because several of my fellow military veteran friends had relocated there. One of those friends was Raymond (Ray Jack) Jackson.

He taught me that one American dollar was worth approximately four Colombian pesos. In other words, the cost of living was extraordinarily lower in Colombia than in America. One of my friends said, "Otis, isn't that exciting? Man, when are you coming to visit and hang out with me and some other military friends in Medellin?" "Man," I said, "you know I don't speak Spanish. I have not studied Spanish since I was in the ninth grade! Neither have I traveled anywhere in South America." But Otis! Man, I speak Spanish fluently. I have studied Spanish at the college in Aurora."

Since I did not speak Spanish, I hesitated to accept my friend's invitation to visit Medellin. Incidentally, he retired from the United States Air Force as a commissioned officer and from the United States Post Office. My friend is originally from Baltimore, Maryland. This means he is a diehard Baltimore Ravens Football fan. He talks continually about his famous football team and his devoted family. Although he is twice divorced, my friend talks proudly about his children and his loving mother. She is now deceased, but she became disgruntled with the abuse she suffered from my friend's father.

Now, my friend and I met initially when I lived and worked in Aurora, Colorado. At that time, I was employed at the Department of Veterans Affairs in Denver but lived in Aurora. My home was located nearly twenty-five miles from my place of employment. Also, while residing in Colorado, I became a leader within The Retired Enlisted Association (TREA) Chapter 3. For several years, I was selected and elected as TREA chaplain.

As a chaplain, I had the opportunity to connect and meet my friend. He was a long-time member of TREA who also enjoyed dual citizenship in America and Colombia. Whenever he traveled from America to Colombia and was cleared through the Colombian Immigration Service, my friend was treated as a citizen of Colombia. While I traveled through the line for all foreigners, he went through the Colombian citizens' line and cleared immigration long before I did.

During my two-week visit to Medellin, I lived with him. He mentored me through the dos and don'ts of the city. He insisted I give only coins, not pesos, to the many indigent people lining the city streets. I saw the great tragedy of how the people there lived and survived. There was no great abundance of employers for people to obtain respectful wage-paying jobs to support themselves and their families. Neither did a safety net exist there like Social Security. The people made it the best way that they could.

I came to understand that the oldest profession in the world—prostitution—was thriving. Prostitution is legal. But, most importantly, I became more sensitive and sympathetic toward those who were prostitutes. It was the only way for single women with children and other family members to provide for their households.

I understand you were once employed as a dancer at a nightclub, but you were not a prostitute. Instead, you were doing what any loving parent does. It is too provide and take care of her or his children.

Moreover, as you know, I am a preacher. I have been in the ministry for more than fifty (50) years. Nonetheless, I used to look at you and anyone else who danced in a nightclub with some disdain. You see, at one time, I was a sanctimonious kind of preacher. I prayed the same kind of prayer that the Pharisee prayed at his church: "Lord, I thank you that I am not lacking other sinners. I prayed and give my tithes and offerings." However, since I have seen how other people live in Colombia and throughout the world, I now pray differently. "Lord, please have mercy on me. I am a sinner".

Also, the founders of the Black Lives Matter Movement (BLM) have raised my consciousness regarding LGBTQ issues and concerns. This movement articulates the social justice concerns of the masses and not the classes. This is the same thing that the Old Testament prophets and, yes, what Martin Luther King Jr. did with the civil rights movement that he helped to lead. Subsequently, it has likewise come to my attention that you may have some LGBTQ sensibilities and predispositions.

Well, please allow me to say this. I know that it is beyond the shadow of a doubt that same-sex relationship is something that is not new. Same-sex relationships have existed throughout human history. So, regardless of whatever your sexual orientation may be, I must say that I love you. I am incredibly proud of your achievements and accomplishments. As a single-parent Mother, you raised some respectful and wonderful children. I challenge you and our relatives and friends to become more politically engaged. Develop an understanding that God is bigger and more significant than anything. Continue to embrace the social and political change that will benefit humankind.

Chapter 6

MY LETTER TO MY BROTHER, ATTORNEY TERRY R. CLAYTON: ON CRIMINAL JUSTICE REFORM

I am five and a half years older than you. I remember the day that Daddy and Mother brought you home as if it was yesterday. You were wrapped in a pink-and-white baby blanket and dressed in baby clothes. When I saw you, I said, "Wh" in the hell is this baby? I know damn well that he cannot be my brother!" Y"u were skinny and long for your size. But your skin color was rather shocking and disturbing. I thought, *I know damn well this baby cannot be my brother. He looks like a White American baby. Has MomMommaen playing around when Dad was not around?* Then, nearly two years later, our baby brother was born; he also looked different. He was a bouncing baby boy whowith darkerin color and complexion wern our other siblings. But the years have passed, and I hear our sisters say, "Yo" and our younger brother look alike. However, "I "ay in response, "Bu" I am the good-looking one!"

"In all seriousness, I acknowledge that I do not have any medical training. Medical doctors have a more sensible explanation for the different skin color shades among African Americans. However, I have hypothesized why this happens. It is that our ancestors were raped and taken advantage of when owned by their slave masenslaversour parents may be of the same skin color, the genes of the former slave mastersenslavers But, year after year, it seemed that I was having one sister and brother after the other. Our parents worked during the day while we lived at 13 West Geeter Road in the Geeter Subdivision. While they worked, they relied on Betty, Edward, Faye, and me to watch out for Rickey, you, La Shun, Myra, and Sandra. And our next-door neighbors, including Aunt Dump (Rosie Lee Clayton-Ray), her husband, Uncle John Henry (John Henry Ray, Sr.) Ray and other neighbors would also watch and take care of all care for us alld daddy were at worDaddykewise, my parents did the same thing for our other neighbors. We lived in a neighborhood that symbolized that it truly takes a village to raise a child.

I looked forward to each evening that Daddy came home from work. He was employed at the Navy Yard Cotton-Compress Company in our young adolescent years. It was located, as I recall, along the southeast corner of Lauderdale and Mallory. When Daddy came through the door, he often said, "Wh"re is my Puddin?"

"I never knew why I was called Puddin. So, one day, when I was visiting MomMomma asked, "Mo" Mommahy did you name me Puddin? You must have wanted me to be born as a girl. "M" ma said, "I "iddidn'tve you the nickname Puddin. Your daddy gave you thDaddyme." *W"w*, I said to myself. *Daddy is now deceased and resting in the arms of God, but he is speaking to me from his grave when I am nearly seventy years old!"*

"When Daddy came in the evenings, he customarily watched the CBS Evening News featuring Walter Cronkite. We were one of the few families with a television in our neighborhood. As a child, I sat in his lap as we watched the news before eating the dinner that momMommad prepared. I remember hearing Walter Cronkite say, "Good Evening. I am Walter Cronkite, and I have your evening news." I"distinctly remember watching the news about the abduction and murder of Emmitt Till in Money, Mississippi, less than two hundred miles south of our home in Memphis. This horrified and terrified Momma, Daddy, and our entire community. Daddy, Uncle John Ray, and other men talked about Emmitt Till. They may not have been active members of our family church, the New Nonconnah Missionary Baptist Church, but they were Prince Hall or Freemason members. Uncle John Henry, a Freemason, said to Daddy, "Bo", I think we must ask the worshipful master and other members to give money to the Emmitt Till family."

"At one time, Daddy worked alongside Granddaddy Luther Murphy at Firestone Rubber and Tire Company. I do not know how long he worked there, but I do know that Daddy went to work for the Navy Yard Cotton-Compress Company (NYCCC). He knew how to work with cotton for any number of reasons, especially. He had experience with preparing cotton for the market with his father, PaPa (Silas Clayton Sr.), his siblings, and other relatives on the Clayton Family Farm. It was located approximately eight to ten miles south of Memphis in Hernando, Mississippi.

Daddy would talk with me, however, about the difficulties that he had while working for NYCCC. I can hear him insisting, "Puddin, those White damn crackers at NYCCC will not promote me. They keep hiring White boys young enough to be my sons. Then, they ask me to train them on the job and tell them what to do as a supervisor. I am tired of doing this daily, weekly and month after month. I want you to go to school and get yourself a good education. I do not want you to have to go through this. Promise me that you will attend school for the best education possible."

""Yes", Daddy, I will do that." This was my typical reply. Sometime after that, although he continued to work at NYCCC, Daddy decided that he must do what was necessary to create additional income. He became a businessman, a bootlegger of corn whiskey, and a gambler. He sold corn whiskey in the evening and on weekends. In addition, he hosted crap games at our home on weekends. Yes! He began to generate additional income. Unfortunately, Daddy's businesses put him in jeopardy with law enforcement.

Momma did not want Daddy to take me anytime he drove south across the Tennessee state line to Mississippi to pick up his corn whiskey. He would pay his supplier, take his empty five-gallon jug out of the trunk of our car, and swap it for a full five-gallon jug. Then Daddy and I would drive back north back across the Mississippi and Tennessee state line.

On one of these occasions, the Mississippi state troopers spotted our car and began to follow us. Daddy drove, and I sat in the front passenger seat. Looking over my left shoulder, I saw two White Mississippi state troopers. Daddy was driving his black-and-white hump-back 1949 Chevrolet

Pontiac; they were driving a black, four-door Ford. They wore wide-brimmed hats. As their car put pull up, Daddy said out loud, "God damn it! It is that crooked ass Hop Dirtien!" The police car drove up on our passenger side with the window rolled down and the siren blaring. "Boy", pull your God damned car over to the side," shouted the officer. (Remember that our Father's nick name was Boy)

Daddy pulled to the ride side of Highway 51 north of Walls, Mississippi. We had been headed for the Tennessee state line. He stopped at a familiar-looking service station and restaurant along the highway. We had stopped there before for gas and food. At any rate, Hop Dirtien walked up to the passenger side where I was sitting. Daddy said, "Pu"din, roll down your window."

"Hop Dirtien spoke to my father: "Boy, I told your ass to slow down several miles back down the road. I could have shot the tires out of your God damned car. Get your ass out. Raise up your hands and open up the trunk of this here God damned car."

"When Daddy opened the trunk of his car, Hop Dirtien stated, "Go" damn, Boy, look what we got here. I need to arrest your Black ass and impound your God damned car. But you need to call someone to get this little boy. Who in the hell is he? Is he your boy?"

"Daddy said, "Ye", Hop Dirtien, he is my son. Can I use the telephone in the restaurant to call my father, Silas Clayton Sr.? I know he will come and get my son." Fortunately, this was a Saturday morning and not a Sunday morning. Otherwise, PaPa and Momma (Bloss as PaPa called her) would have been at the Mount Olive Missionary Baptist Church worship service. The church was a few miles from the family home across the Tennessee-Mississippi state line. Daddy informed PaPa what had happened, and PaPa picked me up and took me home to Momma.

When PaPa and I arrived home, he had a conversation with our Momma. Elizabeth," Papa said, "Bloss and I cannot keep rescuing you and Boy. I cannot count the times we have used our hard-earned money to help you and Boy. And the primary reason that we have helped you all is because of our grandchildren. These children did not ask to come into the world. However, it is not my or Bloss' business to care for our children. You and Boy are going to have to do better. Otherwise, you may lose these children, your house, and your property."

Fields Road/Cook Road Location

Daddy and Momma eventually lose our house at 13 West Geeter Road. It was the house where most of us were born. Without a house, we became gypsies and vagabonds for the next twenty-five years. After those years, we had grown up. We were all women and men. Although you were in college, we came together to help Momma purchase her house on 1795 Wendy Drive.

But, before that moving to 1795, our family residences varied. Remember! We had moved from 13 West Geeter Road to the near the Boxtown Community on Fields Road. Nonetheless, during this period, we experienced increased drama, confusion, and difficulties within our family. At that time, I played basketball as a Geeter School Junior High basketball team member. But, for transportation from practice to home on Fields Road, I had to rely on my basketball coach, Mr. Carruthers. I became a young star basketball player.

When we lived on Geeter Road, I always worked out and played basketball with older basketball players. For the most part, many of them played basketball on the Geeter High School junior and senior basketball teams. They included guys like Melvin Staten, Willie Lee Mackey, and Willie (Pee Pee) Wilson, several older basketball players. They were like big brothers to me. They were always concerned about my well-being and my future development as a top-notch basketball player. So, these guys adopted and mentored me from the first through eighth grades.

During that period, Momma worked as a maid for some White people in Whitehaven during the day. I do not recall their name. Then, during the evening, she worked at the neighborhood Dairy Queen Restaurant. Pee Pee, Willie Lee, Melvin, and others advised her that I needed to exercise good judgment and discretion about Coach Carruthers. Although he coached the junior high school basketball team, Coach Carruthers was a teacher and was the father of two small girls.

But there was something unusual about him. Long story short, my mother was told, "Ms" Elizabeth, Coach Carruthers is a closet homosexual who took advantage of young boys who were naïve and gullible. Yes, Puddin is one of his best basketball players, but he needs to keep his distance from Carruthers."

"Momma did pass on to me what she had been told. The older basketball players also told me that, although Coach Carruthers was married and had children, I should stay away from him. He was trying to mess up the minds of young boys. They advised me not to let my guard down; I should not allow Mr. Carruthers to touch my body, especially my private parts. I remained always mindful and vigilant regarding the insight and advice of Momma my older basketball brothers and dear friends.

When we moved to this Fields Road residence, Coach Carruthers made direct and explicit sexual advantages towards me. _____, my friend lived four houses east of Coach Carruthers home was on Whitehaven Lane. In short, they lived on the same street where Alvin lived. So, it seemed reasonable for Carruthers to take Alvin home last from our basketball practices,

This was quite the contrary. Instead, after each of basketball practice, Coach Carruthers took my friend Alvin home first. Then he drove me home last. He asked me to ride with him in the front seat. Each time he attempted to touch me, I said, "Mr." Carruthers, my mother, and some of the Geeter High School basketball players—Melvin Staten, Willie Lee Mackey, and Willie Wilson—told me about you. So, I want you to know that I do not want you or anyone to touch me inappropriately. My Daddy and I will kick your ass or will kick our ass. I do not want you ever to try to touch me."

Hobart Alley/Fill-Up with Billups Location

We moved next from the Field Road location to the Hobart Alley location. Remember! It was right behind the Fill-Up with Billups Service Station location. A see-through iron fence separated the service station from Hobart Alley, but the service station located on Crump Boulevard was always extremely busy. The large Clayborn Holmes Housing Complex was directly across the street. Invariably, many customers stopped purchasing gas, cigarettes, and other items.

At this time, the dysfunctional relationship between our parents reached a boiling point. Daddy's bootlegging days had concluded. So, his way to make additional money beyond his day job was solely through gambling with dice and going to the dog track in West Memphis, Arkansas. However, at that time, Mommas now working two jobs. She cooked at a restaurant downtown on Beale Street in the evening and on weekends.

Also, she worked during the day at the Memphis Furniture Company. It was a dangerous company to work for because there was no labor union. Meanwhile, Daddy work habits became more erratic. He would work during the day, gamble, and play with the dogs in the evenings. Every Friday morning, he would go to work; he was paid on Friday evenings. But, He would not return home until late Sunday night or even Monday morning when he would have to go back to work. Sadly, each time he returned home, Daddy was always broke.

At that time, Momma would ask, "Boy"! Where is your money? Our children did not ask to come into this world. You and I are responsible for them. They need food, clothes, and shelter. They need supplies for school and other necessities." Daddy would try to ignore Momma would say, "Elizabeth. Let me alone. Get out of my face". Momma was only five foot three, and she weighed no more than 150 fifty pounds.

On the other hand, Daddy was six-three and weighed nearly 240 pounds. Nevertheless, Momma would not allow her disadvantage in height and weight deter her from saying what needed to be said. She again and again told Daddy, "Boy! Where is your money?" Then, our parents would physically fight.

Now, when Betty, Edward, Faye, and I were younger, we would not intervene anytime Daddy and Momma got into fisticuffs. Momma would call the Memphis police. When they arrived, the police would ultimately make a report. Momma would always have some bruises somewhere on her face, hands, or body. The police would arrest Daddy and take him to jail for spousal abuse. Later that evening or the next day Momma, PaPa, or some other relative or friend would bail him out of jail.

But, when we moved to the Hobart Alley location, our father experienced a rude awakening—several of his children had come of age. Betty, Faye, and I would no longer stand aside while he physically abused and beat down our beloved and caring Momma, yes! We came to our Mother's rescue. She was the parent who always sacrificed her well-being for the benefit of her children. Therefore, for me, she is our beautiful African-American mother. She would give her last dime to her children. So, occasionally, I call her not just Momma also Queen Elizabeth. She is the best mother ever.

About a couple of days later, Daddy went to work at his new job at the Fruehauf Trailer Corporation. It was located on Riverside Drive near Interstate 40 West. Herbert McGowan Sr. (Uncle Hebert), who was the husband of Daddy'sster (Aunt Willie Mae), helped him get that job. Unlike his job at the Navy Yard Cotton-Compress Company, his former employer, the job with this company was a union job that provided better wages and insurance benefits for the employees and family members.

Additionally, when Daddy went off to work early one morning, I remember what Momma said to all of us: "I want all of you to go on to school today, but do not come back here. Instead, I want all of you to go to 813 Neptune Street. It will be our new home. I am tired of this mess with your Daddy. All we do is just fuss and fight." The house at 813 Neptune Street is located slightly northeast of here before you get to the railroad tracks and the Feed Mill. Do not go past the railroad tracks. Later this evening, after work, I will be there. But, right now, some friends will help me move our clothes and furniture out of here to Neptune Street."

"I have forgotten how you and our other sisters and brothers made it to our new residence. Momma may have met you all at the Alonzo Locke Elementary School. But, a few weeks later, Daddy located where Momma moved us. He came to the house and tried to talk to her, but the die had been cast. Momma remarked, "Bo", I have had enough. I can do bad by myself. I can do without the neglect and spousal abuse I receive from you. I work two jobs now that provide enough income to keep a roof over our children'sads, buy enough food, pay other expenses, and purchase other material things. But I am going to juvenile court to request your child support payments."

"Shortly after that, Momma purchased a station wagon. She taught me how to drive in that car, and she took me to get my Tennessee driver' license. Although she and Daddy had separated and were going through divorce proceedings, there are just a few other things to mention about what was occurring within our family. Our household experienced some other unforeseen challenges.

Momma's manufacturing job at Memphis Furniture Company was extremely grueling and dangerous. One day, she said, "Puddin, I have injured both my hands and need surgery. I want you to know that my job is not union-paying. I will be unable to work for a while. I don't know how long it will take me to get some Social Security disability benefits. I want you also to know that, sometimes in life when it rains, it also pours. Betty, your big sister, is pregnant going into her senior year of high school. So, I am going to need your help financially".

"Remember! Edward came back home. From the third grade until his second semester in the tenth grade, he had lived in the home of Granddaddy (Luther Murphy Sr.) and Little Momma (Ether Ray Murphy) along with _____ (our youngest maternal uncle).

Granddaddy said, "Edward has simply lost his mind. He has become extremely disruptive, runs away from home, is failing in school, and has begun to smoke. Ethel and I have become too old to deal with Edward's terrible behavior. So, before I hurt him, I think we should bring him home to you all". Meanwhile, although he later obtained a part-time job after school, Edward became another mouth to feed. But, before coming back home, Edward had been a musician for the Geeter High School marching band. He played the drums.

Since I was still attending high school during the day, I needed to locate a full-time job to provide income to help Momma provide for our household. But I needed a night-time job. I would work it after school. Further, this meant that I had to stop playing high school basketball. Basketball was truly my first love. I had played it in the community and for my school most of my life. But I thought and said to myself, *My Momma and my siblings are more important than playing the game of high school basketball. I must demonstrate the mindset, faith, and determination to quit playing basketball and get a full-time job.*

Melvin _____ was a fellow high school classmate and friend. When neither of us was working at our part-time job after school, we hung out. We had become like two peas in a pot. Melvin's parents and siblings lived in a brick house in a small residential community along the rail tracks on Porter Street directly across from the Lemoyne Gardens Public Housing. Melvin's home became, in some ways, my home away from home. His parents and sisters accepted me as a family member.

One evening, while I was sitting in my friend's home talking, I asked his sister Sophia about employment opportunities where she worked. Sophia had graduated years earlier from Booker T. Washington High School. A few months after graduation, she became pregnant and had a baby, but Sophia's parents embraced her and her baby son. Sophia and her baby continued to live in the family home. While Sophia worked, her parent's took care of her son. Sophia worked during the day for the Southern Central Paper Company (SCPC). It was located less than a mile from the Johnson family home and two streets over from our home on Neptune. It was union-organized, paid excellent wages, and provided insurance benefits for the employees.

Sophia said, "Yes", Crookethead, my employer is accepting applications. I suggest you go there on Dudley Street, sit at the personnel office, complete an application, and use my name as a reference." I did what Sophia said immediately. I received a telephone call a few days later. At the tender age of sixteen, I became a full-time employee at the SCPC, working from three in the afternoon until eleven at night. My new job at SCPC was a blessing in disguise in so many ways. But, most importantly, it meant that I had, by necessity, grown up, become a man, and put away childish things.

Chezita Garden Location (Now Called Hillview Village Apartments)

Shortly after I obtained employment at SCPC, Momma was accepted as a tenant at the Chezita Gardens Apartments. This was a Memphis public housing development located ten miles southeast of Neptune. It was also near a residential community along Interstate 40 Highway East. Ours was an extremely spacious apartment with central heat and air, four bedrooms, a large living room, a kitchen, and one large bathroom. Momma had her bedroom. The boys and the sisters had their own separate bedrooms and storage areas.

At about the same time, our Father (Daddy) had become a new employee in Saginaw, Michigan. He worked for General Motors Corporation. Now, before he relocated to Saginaw, Michigan, Daddy dropped in occasionally to see us. One day, when he came by, I requested a meeting with our parents in the living room. They sat on the couch, and I sat on a stool before them.

I stated, "Daddy and Momma, I am glad you allowed me to talk to both of you. You may not want to hear what I am about to say, but I must let you know what's my mind. Your children need both of you. We are growing up like weeds. I go to school full-time, and after school, I work from three in the afternoon to eleven in the evening. Momma picks me up after work sometimes; otherwise, I catch a ride home with my coworkers. Sometimes, my girlfriend' parents, Mr. and Mrs. Williams, pick me up and drive me home. I am saving some money and hope to buy my own car soon. Now, I have never been an African-American male teenager before. I am going through so many things. Daddy, I need to talk to you about how to deal with young women. Betty has a small baby now. Before I complete my education, I do not want to make a mistake and become a young father. I got all this hair growing on my body. My voice keeps getting lower. I must, from time to time, shave hair off my face."

"Before Daddy moved north to Saginaw, he needed to show his birth certificate to become employed at General Motors there. When he received a copy of his certificate, he was suddenly surprised by what he saw. The name on his birth certificate was Aaron Clayton and not Otis Clayton. Next, he took a copy over to the home of PaPa and Momma (Bloss) to show them. Daddy said, "Papa and Momma, see the name on my birth certificate? It is Aaron Clayton and not Otis Clayton."

"PaPa said, "Fool, I need you to listen to me. At your birth, Bloss and I knew what we named you. We named you Otis Clayton and not Aaron Clayton. In those days, when you were born, Black women were not allowed to give birth in the hospital, so the midwife delivered Black babies. Now, the midwife put the name Aaron Clayton on your birth certificate because she only knew that you were the grandson of Aaron Clayton. Now, I am afraid that if you begin to use the name Aaron Clayton, you will mess up the name of Aaron Clayton as you have done with Otis Clayton."

Later, Daddy came back to talk to Momma and us. He stated, "Elizabeth, I got a job now working for General Motor Corporation. I will make more money to help my family live better. I will be a member of one of the best unions—the United Auto Workers (UAW). It provides the best insurance to pay for medical care for all employees and their family members. We can have a better life there in Saginaw, Michigan."

"Momma made the following reply: "Bo"! You and I got married at a young age. I was fifteen years old, and you were almost nineteen. I had all our children year after year. We had a new house built at thirteen West Geeter Road. It is there that most of our children were born. We lived in that house for over fifteen years. Then, although you worked at the Navy Yard Cotton-Compress Company, you started to bootleg corn whiskey and gamble and get into trouble with the police. The only time that I was arrested was when the police came into our house with an arrest warrant, found corn whiskey, and arrested me. We got behind in paying our house note. My Daddy helped us to pay our past due house notes. Mr. Silas and Bloss (Mrs. Roberia) helped us pay our past house notes. But, after living there for over fifteen years, we lost that house on Geeter Road. Since losing our home, we have moved these children to four different locations.

But we are doing much better now. We have a comfortable place to live. Of course, since we did not make it here in Memphis, I do not believe we will make it in Saginaw, Michigan."

Now, When I graduated from Booker T. Washington High School, like Momma and most Americans, I did not favor the Vietnam War. I believed that it was an unjust war. So, I obtained a military deferment so that I did not have to serve in the armed forces temporarily.

At seventeen of age, our brother, _____ graduated from high school and decided to volunteer for the United States Air Force. He completed boot camp and technical school and was assigned to active duty at the Minot Air Force Base in Minot, North Dakota. Edward had trained as a security policeman, but after his arrival, he received military orders for Vietnam. He said to me, "Puddin, I am ready to go. I will primarily provide a protection force for my base."

"I replied, "Edward, you know my position regarding the Vietnam War. I am not in favor of our participation in it. Black soldiers are being killed a higher number than White soldiers, but, at the same time, they are unable to vote in America. They are unable to eat at certain restaurants and attend some movie theaters. This is a dynamic that must be changed in America before Black soldiers are sent to Vietnam to fight for someone else freedom in a foreign country.

Walter Simmons Housing Project

I graduated from LeMoyne Owen College, got married, and volunteered for service in the United States Air Force. I was eventually assigned for active duty at the Seymour Johnson Air Force Base in Goldsboro, North Carolina. Then, my family and I were transferred to Little Rock Air Force Base in Jacksonville, Tennessee. My son, _____ was born there. When I completed my active duty, we returned to Memphis to live.

But, unfortunately, Momma's apartment burned down. She had lived there for approximately ten years. Derrick _____, our three-year-old nephew, was playing with a box of matches. In the process, he set the entire apartment blazing. Momma lived for a short time with Betty and her family in another apartment in Chezita Gardens.

I scheduled an appointment with my pastor, _____, at Mount Moriah East Baptist Church. In his office. I said, "Pastor _____, hello. I am thankful that you allowed me to come and have a conversation with you. I know that you are rather busy, so I am happy to share this time with you. My Mother, Elizabeth Clayton, is a member of Boston Baptist Church. As you know, your good friend, Pastor Oris Mays, is her long-time pastor. My mother's apartment was burned down several days ago. One of my nephews was playing with a box of matches and caused the destruction of her apartment in Chezita Garden. She had been living there for more than ten years. I need your help. Can you please help me find a place for my mother to live?"

"I remember it as if it was yesterday. Pastor _____ responded, "Otis, I appreciate you. I know that you and your family are new members here. You are a veteran. You are one of our new preachers here. My long-time members, Deacon Ernest Washington and his wife, Mother Sarah Washington, are some of our most faithful members. They talk highly about you because your wife, Jackie, is one of their godchildren. They helped to raise her. Now, I think even more highly of you because of your desire to help your mother. I have a mother, and if my mother needed anything, I would do what you are doing. So, I will call my good friend, _____, the Memphis Housing Authority executive director, and request that he do whatever possible to help your darling mother locate a place to live."

"Several days later, a Memphis Housing Authority representative contacted Momma advising her to visit the Walter Simmons Apartments Office near Lamar Avenue for an apartment walk-through. She did as was suggested and later moved into her new apartment.

Wendy Drive: Finally, a Home for Momma

I was required to return to Memphis from active military duty. So, my wife and I and our children, moved to East Memphis. My ___worked as an apartment manager; consequently, we were able to live on the property in an apartment without paying rent; we paid only for utilities. One day I told her, "___"___ I learned that, since a union with your employer does not represent you, your manager or the owner of your company may decide to fire you one day without any warning. So, I believe it would be prudent for us to purchase our own house and let my brother Rickey live in it while you have your job here. Now, Mrs. Gordon is retired, and her husband is deceased. She now wants to live in a senior citizen high-rise apartment, so she had placed her own house at 1785 Wendy Drive on the market. Yes! It is located directly across the dead-end street from your parents' home. Never mind where that house is located. Nonetheless, we need to buy Mrs. Gordon house. Again, honestly, we never know what your employer will do. You do not have a union to represent you. We can use my veterans benefit to purchase that house for us."

"At first, my wife _____vehemently opposed my suggestion. "I does not want to live near Momma and Daddy," she said. "Living there will probably cause all kinds of problems for us. Momma and Daddy may try to get into our business".

"But I continued to insist that she needed to take another look at my suggestion. "You know that I go to school during the day. I work at night. Since I am in the Air National Guard, I do, from time to time, leave town for military duty. It would a good idea for you to live closer to your parents; they may be able to help us and babysit for our children, _____. Also, our daughter can go to Alcy Elementary School, which is right around the corner from that house." _"____My wife finally agree with me, and I used my veterans' benefit to purchase our first home—1785 Wendy Drive.

Sometime shortly after we purchased our house, the house next door at 1795 Wendy Drive came available for purchase through foreclosure. I saw the for-sale sign on the yard sign listing a contact number. I called the number and express interest: "Si", I am Otis Clayton Sr. My wife and I own the property next door at 1785 Wendy Drive. What is the selling price for your property at 1795 Wendy Drive?"

He replied, "I "m a property investor and want any interested buyer to give me twelve thousand dollars and you be responsible he mortgage balance. I need six thousand in thirty days or less, and I need six thousand within the next six months or less. Then, you can finance the mortgage balance on your own".

I gave him a deposit to express my interest, and he granted me thirty days to get back to him. If you recall, Momma and Sandra, our baby sisters, were living in the Walter Simmons Apartments. Jackie and I discussed how we could provide financial support toward the $12,000 balance. I had recently won my suit against the United Parcel Service (UPS) with the United States Labor Relations Board. So, my wife, _____, and I had $6,000 we could give toward the balance. Then, I called Daddy and all our siblings. Although Daddy and Momma were divorced, he sent $2,500 to liquidate the $12,000 balance.

Chapter 7

MY LETTER TO REVEREND EDWARD LEE THOMPSON: COMMUNITY ORGANIZING

A Conscientious Objector:
Notably a Man of Principle

Our mutual friend and brother, Oliver Peyton, and I talk periodically whenever I visit Memphis to spend quality time with my beloved mother. Oliver and his brother, Reginald, moved up from Hollis Springs, Mississippi. Like you, they graduated from Christian Brothers College and opened a Peyton Realty Company business. They have operated that business for over fifty years, and it has become highly productive. They now have two office locations: South Memphis in the Whitehaven Community and East Memphis in the Riverdale Community.

I met Oliver over forty years ago when I performed the marriage ceremony of my brother, Terry, and his first wife,_____. My brother, his wife, and Juanita, Oliver's wife, were law students at Southern University School of Law in Baton Rouge, Louisiana. At that time, Juanita and Oliver had agreed to have a long-distance marriage relationship. They had two sons, whom Ollie cared for while Juanita was away attending law school.

When Juanita graduated from law school, they had one more child—Juanita (Nita) Lavern Peyton Jr. Meanwhile, I would often visit the Peyton family's beautiful riverfront home. It was located on Mud Island to hang out with them and rub shoulders with some of the who's who of Memphis who occasionally dropped by their home. These Memphis personalities include Judge H. T. (Hosea) Lockett, State Senator Rosco Dickson, Dr. W.W. Herrington, and other dignitaries.

Sometime within this time frame, their daughter, Juanita, was killed tragically in a car accident on Riverside Drive in Memphis. Oliver was the driver of their vehicle when Nita was dead. Juanita could, however, never get over the loss of Nita, and she may have pointed the finger at Oliver for causing that terrible car accident. They received marriage counseling, but Juanita could never come to terms with the death of their Nita. She died prematurely sometime after that because of mental and medical issues.

Oliver's oldest son, _____., has been in and out of several jails. A few years ago, his oldest daughter graduated from Tennessee State University while he was out of jail. I attended the graduation and the reception held in her honor. Then, not too long after that, Oliver's son was arrested for driving drunk without a license. He is now incarcerated in Mississippi. Oliver Sr., from time to time, tells me the story of his son.

I have mentioned your name since Oliver Sr., and I have been talking. I ask, "Oliver, when was the last time you heard from our dear friend, Reverend Edward Lee Thompson? "Clayton," he said the last time I asked, "man, I have not heard from him in years. But I occasionally see him and his wife, _____, at a Manassas High School Alma function. He, his wife, and his brothers are all staunch, diehard supporters and boosters of Manassas High School. Eddie _____ and I attended Christian Brothers College with my brother, Reginald. Eddie Lee, Raenette___ (now Judge _____), and her husband are graduates of Manassas High School. They were all exceptional students in school.

Eddie Lee was so brilliant that he earned his degree in Mathematics. I also must inform you that Eddie Lee was just a chip off the block like his father. He was the long-time principal at Carver High School. But he was also a devoted Christian and African Methodist Episcopal Church (AME) member. So, Eddie Lee's father was a man of principle. And, if he believed in something, he would take it and stand for what he believed in. Heaven and hell could not move him from his position.

So, unlike his father and other relatives, Eddie Lee took a stand to oppose induction into the Army. He did agree with the Vietnam War and declared himself as a conscious objector. He spent time in prison because Reverend Eddie Thompson has always been a man of principle. He will always take a stand against something he believes is unjust.

Confessions of a Student Crush: On Your Future Wife

Andrew Davis and I were high school classmates and Booker T. Washington High School graduates. We both lived in a Memphis housing project. I lived in Chezita Gardens Apartments, and he lived in LeMoyne Gardens. Andrew had a twin brother named Anthony. Their first cousin, _____, was my girlfriend, and years later, she became my wife. One day, while walking down the street, I met her _____when she came to visit Andrew and his family in LeMoyne Gardens.

Like me, Andrew and Anthony were constantly working to make a living. They worked in the evening and on weekends at Liberty Cash Grocery Store; I worked at night for Southern Central Paper Company. However, immediately after high school, Anthony got into trouble with the authorities and went to prison for several years. His incarceration was extremely difficult for Andrew and their entire family. The income that Anthony had provided to help his mother, whom we called Aunt Betsy, was no longer there.

Andrew and I were accepted and enrolled as freshmen at LeMoyne Owen College. We were glad to become students. We had received the military deferment that prevented us from being called up to fight in the Vietnam War. But, with that in mind, we were not necessarily interested in college. We established a daily routine that reflected this disinterest. Almost every day at noon, we left campus, had lunch, drank liquor, and smoked marijuana cigarettes.

Terry _____was one of our former high school classmates who was a dope dealer and hustler. He sometimes sold marijuana on campus or down on the corner of Mississippi Walker, which was less than a quarter of a mile down the street from LeMoyne College. "Hi, Terry. How is it going, man?" was my customary greeting when I saw him.

Terry sometimes replied, "Crookedhead, what's up with you? Crookedhead, you crazy motherfucker. You know you got no damn business trying to go to college. Nigger, you can't even spell college."

I would answer, "Terry, please don't sell me any bad weed. In all honesty, you are a jealous nigger. You did not want to be in college pursuing a college education."

My first year of college was somewhat of a disaster. I lost my National Defense student grant, which was money that I did not have to repay. I failed to maintain a C average and above to keep that grant. Instead, I argued, sadly, only a 1.78 grade point average.

During my first year at LeMoyne Owen College, confession was good for the soul and one bright spot. I earned my highest grades. I took a sociology class from one of the most beautiful professors on campus, Maxine _____ . Although I failed English composition and literature that year, I did my best in her class, given my circumstances and situation. I was always prepared, attentive, and alert to participate in class discussions. Oh, no, I was not alone in my admiration for Maxine. My male classmates sometimes say before and after class, "Professor Maxine _____ is one of the most gorgeous-looking women in the universe. Her intelligence, complexion, height, teeth, and hair are all God-given gifts. When God made Professor Maxine Seaborn, God threw away the mold. There are no other women like her."

Reaching Out to Help a Struggling Student at MTS

When I became a student at MTS, I found the experience to be one of my life's most memorable and intellectually challenging. At that time, after completing my four years of active duty in the Air Force, my family and I relocated to Memphis. I was in my late twenties, married, and the father of two children. I worked two jobs and was new in the ministry. Nonetheless, I came face to face with a reality I knew existed. I possessed an inadequate and inferior educational background for conducting graduate research and writing exercises.

Before I became a student at MTS, I had completed degrees from Central Michigan University and LeMoyne Owen College. I had earned a bachelor's degree and a master of arts degree. However, before beginning my studies at MTS, I had been required to write only one research paper. Now, in all honesty, I composed that research paper with the help of my classmate, Alvin Sinclair. Alvin and I had known one another since we were students at Geeter Elementary School. Unlike me, Alvin came from a small, stable middle-class environment. His father was a federal government employee, and his mother was an elementary teacher at Geeter Elementary School.

When we met at MTI, I had no idea that so much reading, writing, and critical thinking would be required. But you encouraged and helped me intellectually. Like Alvin, you possessed research and writing skills I did not have. You came from a family with a college education, beginning as early as your parents, Richard and Lucy.

Although she was not a schoolteacher, Lucy graduated from Owen College. Richard Thomas served in Memphis schools for more than forty-five years. He was the distinguished principal at Carver High School for more than thirty years alone and at other schools.

With your educational background and foundation, I knew it was pivotal that I develop a friendship with you to get a better feel for what I must do to become a successful student. If you recall, I sometimes followed you around the MTS library to learn research and writing skills from you. In the process, I learned from you how to expand my reading appetite and reading horizons comprehensively and cogently.

You and I took several courses together from Professor Joe Ben Irby. I truly learned a great deal from him because I aspired to become a professor in theology like Professor Irby. But, unlike us, Professor Irby was a theologian in the Anglo-American Reformed cultural heritage tradition. This meant that his theological views, as an Anglo-American, did not necessarily reflect our African-American theological perspective. On one hand, you were from the African Methodist Episcopal Church tradition. Your congregations were connected throughout the Episcopal jurisdiction.

On the other hand, I was from the Black Baptist perspective. We were more congregational regarding what was done directly through the individual congregation. Nonetheless, we shared and embraced an African-American theological perspective because of our cultural heritage.

In our class with Professor Irby, I saw how you used African-American theological sources to make specific points. Likewise, I employed the same theological process.

Your methodology proved to be promising and beneficial for both of us. After our studies at MTS, we both graduated with academic honors. I will always remain eternally grateful for the way you helped me adapt to the academic environment at MTS. In the process, I was able to strive and ultimately persevere.

Opening Your Pulpit to Help Me Develop as a Preacher

At MTS, I attended class during the day, worked at night, served in the Tennessee Army National Guard, and served as an associate minister at Central Baptist Church. Then, after graduating from MTS, I became a graduate philosophy student at Memphis State University (now called the University of Memphis). I studied there for three years until I earned a master of arts in philosophy. Then, I studied philosophy and theology briefly at Boston University. So, while researching and preparing for ministry, I had limited opportunities to develop my skills as a preacher.

You undertook a different trajectory to develop your skills as a preacher. You became a student pastor for several AME congregations during your years at MTS. I came as a guest to hear you preach on several occasions.

Several years after graduating from Memphis State University and completing a period of preparation for pulpit ministry, I became the Antioch Baptist Church (ABC) pastor in Batesville, Mississippi. The ABC congregation was sixty miles from my home in Memphis. I served that congregation for more than one year. But, during that period of pulpit ministry, I finally obtained the opportunity to hone and develop my skills as a preacher and orator. I learned that to become an influential preacher, I must continue studying constantly and work hard at preaching. Preaching itself is a never-finished art. Additionally, the most effective and renowned preachers spend time getting to know their congregations. Preaching involves teaching the scriptures, visiting congregants at home and in the hospital, marrying their children, counseling them, and burying their dead.

After my tenure at ABC, I became interested in becoming the pastor of a self-supporting congregation. The Reverend Dr. Reuben Green suggested I apply to the vacant pulpit at First Baptist Church, Capitol Hill, in Nashville, Tennessee. Pastor Green had been a colleague and friend of the nationally known Reverend Kelly Miller Smith Sr, the former pastor. Besides being a famous preacher, Pastor Smith has been a dear friend and lieutenant of Dr. Martin Luther King Jr. in the civil rights movement. However, after his death, his congregation formed a search committee to help locate the next pastor. So, I made an application, attached Pastor Green's letter of recommendation, and mailed it to the committee at First Baptist Church.

When I mailed my application, I had earned four degrees: a bachelor of arts, a master of divinity, and two master of arts. The search committee at First Baptist Church, Capitol Hill, rejected my application because I did not possess a doctoral degree. The former pastor, Pastor Kelly Miller Smith, included only a bachelor of divinity degree (or master of divinity degree) from Morehouse College in Atlanta, Georgia; nonetheless, the congregation had decided that the next pastor of First Baptist Church, Capitol Hill, must possess a doctoral degree because the next pastor would also become an adjunct professor at the Vanderbilt University School of Divinity.

I was deeply saddened and dejected that my application to become a candidate by the First Baptist Church, Capitol Hill, had been denied; after all, I was an educated preacher. So, I did some soul-searching. I also discussed with my wife, our children, family members, and Pastor Green what happened with my First Baptist Church, Capitol Hill, application. Afterward, I decided that as we advanced, my application to fill a vacancy at the next church would not be denied because I had not earned a doctoral degree. I applied to pursue a doctoral degree at the Vanderbilt University School of Divinity and was accepted. I relocated temporarily to Nashville to date and completed my doctoral degree.

When I relocated to metropolitan Nashville, I realized you had become a pastor of two AME congregations—Allen Chapel AME Church in Murfreesboro and Lee Chapel AME Church in Nashville. Meanwhile, although I am not a minister who follows the AME tradition, you invited me to preach sermons to your congregations. This is simply to say that you have supported my development to become a more effective minister and preacher of the Gospel.

Leading a Socially Engaged Ministry: Nashville Organization for Action and Hope (NOAH)

I retired from the Department of Veterans Affairs (Health Administration Center) in Denver, Colorado. To celebrate that event, my family members and some close friends had a worship service and retirement party at my home in Aurora. I paid for the air travel to have my mother, Elizabeth, and my sister, _____, present for this special occasion. However, my mother did not know my retirement celebration was also a surprise—a happy belated eightieth-birthday celebration for her. My mother's birthday was on October 20, but I could not be in Memphis to celebrate with her and other family members. I asked my sister, Betty, not to tell her about the surprise party for her.

Bishop Phillips made special remarks and led us in prayer. Bishop Phillips was the emeritus pastor, and I had accepted him as one of my local fathers in the ministry. Lonnie _____and members of his band provided musical entertainment. Lonnie is the son of a Church of God in Christ (COGIC) pastor in Houston, Texas. He drew in his father's church singing and playing the bass guitar and other musical instruments. Lonnie is also the first cousin of Zee Zee Hill, the famous blues singer. Unlike Zee Zee, Lonnie sings and performs rhythm, blues, and gospel music. Several of his hit songs are "Galveston Bay," "Could It Be Love," "Hard Times," and "Call on Jesus." Previously, I had met Lonnie and members of his band when I saw them perform in downtown Denver, and I invited them to my home to perform. One of Bishop Phillip's church members who owned and operated a catering service provided the food and refreshments for this celebration.

We had a ten-minute interlude after the bishop's prayer, a musical selection by Lonnie, and a food and refreshment service. Bishop Phillips asked for everyone's attention. He informed everyone in attendance that there was a double celebration. He stated, "My son, Dr. Otis Clayton Sr., has retired from the United States Army and the Department of

Veterans Affairs. This is also a belated birthday celebration for his beloved mother, Mother Elizabeth Clayton." Colorado State Senator Rhonda Fields presented my mother with red, pink, and white roses.

Stanley, a Chi Omega Psi Phi Fraternity member, had his young son, Elijah, read the poem, "Mother to Son" by Langton Hughes.

> Well, son, I'll tell you:
> Life for me ain't been no crystal stair.
> It's had tacks in it,
> And splinters,
> And boards torn up,
> And places with no carpet on the floor—
> Bare.
> But all the time
> I'se been a-climbin' on,
> And reachin' landin's,
> And turnin' corners,
> And sometimes goin' in the dark
> Where there ain't been no light.
> So, boy, don't you turn back.
> Don't you set down on the steps.
> 'Cause you finds it's kinder hard.
> Don't you fall now—
> For I'se still goin', honey,
> I'se still climbin',
> And life for me ain't been no crystal stair.

Elizabeth Clayton, my mother, gave brief remarks. She said, "I thank my son, Dr. Otis Clayton Sr., for giving me this surprise happy belated birthday celebration. God has blessed me to travel from Memphis, Tennessee, to Aurora, Colorado, to meet some of my other children. It seems that everywhere Otis and my other children traveled, I gain more adopted children. I want all of you to pray for me because I will keep all of you in prayer. You are all my children."

After my mother's remarks, Bishop Phillips asked me to make a few brief remarks. "Bishop Phillips, Brother Lonnie, my mother, my big sister Betty, and all of you, my sisters, my brothers, and my dear friends, I thank God. You have taken a few hours out of your busy schedules to spend some precious moments with me, my mother, my sisters, and with one another at my home. You did not have to do that, but you did stop by. Now, I do also want you to know that I have been accepted at Canterbury Christ Church University in Canterbury, England, to pursue post-doctoral studies. I will temporarily relocate to Canterbury to study at the first of the year, but I am not moving from Aurora, Colorado."

When I arrived in England and began my studies, everything went well. I met Professor, the chairman of the Humanities Department, and Professor Gabriella, my first reader for my proposed thesis in theology. Nonetheless, less than two years into my studies, I began to experience some medical issues in the form of increasing pain in my lower back and spine area. These issues had been caused by injuries I had received during my previous years of military service. To deal with my injuries, I took a medication called meloxicam, a nonsteroidal anti-inflammatory pain medicine. This drug eventually produced some severe medical side effects. I began to experience internal bleeding, and I was hospitalized for eight days at a nearby hospital.

Upon discharge, I immediately scheduled a flight from London to Nashville, Tennessee. When I arrived, I called the orthopedic surgeon who had recently performed spine surgery on my brother, Terry. I met at the Tri-Star Hospital in Smyrna with Terry, La Shun, Dr. Shibayama, and Dr. Doreen. At the time, Terry and Dr. Doreen were dating. Because of her previous working relationship with Dr. Shibayama, she referred Terry to him for spine surgery.

During Terry's surgery, Dr. Doreen had requested that I offer a prayer. "Lord, I ask you to throw your strong arm of protection around Terry, Dr. Shibayama, and his team. Please keep all of us in your care as we wait patiently for Terry's positive surgical outcome and speedy recovery. In the name of our God who does all things well. Amen!"

Dr. Shibayama said, "Pastor Clayton, now that you have prayed, I also want to pray. Like you, I am a devoted follower of Christ." When he finished praying, I said to myself, *If I ever needed spine surgery, my surgeon would be no other than Dr. Shibayama.*

Approximately two months after my brother's surgery, my time I arrived. Dr. Shibayama obtained the MRI results on my spine. We met in his office to discuss the surgical procedure to replace the ruptured spinal disc in the L-4/L-5 area and tie them together.

Now, strangely, on the morning of the surgery, you arrived at the Tri-Star Hospital in Smyrna, Tennessee, before I did. You and I reminisced and talked about our ministry journey from MTS to the present. Then, right before I was taken into the operating room, Dr. Shibayama and you prayed. "Dear God, thank you for waking us up to see another day, allowing us to drive down the dangerous highways, and make it here safely. We ask you to be with Otis, Dr. Shibayama, his family, and the nurses and staff. Please guide Dr. Shibayama's hands as he performs the needed surgery to provide Otis with some healing. We pray that one day, all your people worldwide will be able to receive the kind of medical attention that Otis is receiving today. In the name of our God, through Jesus Christ, we pray. Amen."

Immediately after spinal surgery, I applied and was granted a medical leave of absence from my studies at Canterbury Christ Church University. I needed this medical leave for rehabilitation after the surgery. During my medical leave, I followed my doctor's advice and relocated temporarily from Nashville to Memphis to live with my sister, _____ for six weeks. It was somewhat challenging to live with my sister; we had not lived under the same roof since we were in our early twenties. However, I carefully followed her advice and counsel to prevent any injuries.

Before I knew it, the six weeks had gone by quickly. Betty and my grand-nephew, _____, her grandson, drove us approximately 250 miles from Memphis, Tennessee, to Smyrna, Tennessee, to Dr. Shibayama's office for my six-week checkup. Dr. Shibayama provided me with a good bill of health. "Otis, you can now return to normal activities in moderation." After receiving this vote of confidence from Dr. Shibayama, I reassessed my situation and circumstances. I became a member of the Mount Zion Baptist Church (entire Gospel), spoke to my mentor, Professor Lewis Baldwin (emeritus professor, Vanderbilt University), and became a member of the Nashville Organization for Action and Hope.

Mount Zion Baptist (MZB) had been looking for another pastor after the death of their previous pastor. I applied to fill that MZB pulpit vacancy but never heard from the pulpit committee. The congregation decided to offer the position of pastor to Reverend Joseph. The pastor was already an associate minister of the MZB congregation and had prepared himself for pastoral leadership. He graduated from Southern University in Baton Rouge, Louisiana, earned a master of divinity from Vanderbilt University School of Divinity, and was a doctoral student at Princeton University.

Incidentally, Pastor Walker and I are also Omega Psi Phi Fraternity Incorporated members. When I became a member of MZB, I said, "Brother Pastor, I want you to know something. Several years ago, when Mount Zion Baptist was seeking another pastor, I made an application. I never heard from the pulpit committee or any congregation member, but I am glad the church made the right decision. The church elected you as the pastor." He laughed at my comment, and so did I.

My mentor, Professor Lewis, and I had a long conversation. He stated, "Brother Otis, I know you lived in Aurora, Colorado. It is a long way from Nashville, Tennessee. Nevertheless, I wish you had called and talked with me before you applied to Canterbury Christ Church University to pursue post-doctoral studies. You already have earned a doctoral degree from one of the best universities in the world. So, why not use the doctoral degree that you already have? You also have a strong background in the discipline of philosophy. I strongly suggest you begin writing, teaching, preaching, and publishing in religion and philosophy."

I also spoke with you about the Nashville Organization for Hope and Action (NOHA). You invited me, the president, to attend a NOHA meeting. I was excited to learn that my brother, Terry, was also working with the other attorneys who were members or associated with NOHA. I was shocked, moreover, that NOHA is a community organization that is designed primarily to fight for social justice for the masses against the classes or the power brokers who are especially concerned about profits over people. NOHA is part of a national faith-based organization called the Gamaliel Foundation. This is undoubtedly meaningful because you are leading a robust community organizing organization that uses faith to make a difference in the lives of every citizen in Metropolitan Nashville-Davidson County.

Chapter 8

LETTER TO MY VANDERBILT UNIVERSITY PROFESSOR, DR. LEWIS BALDWIN: CLIMATE JUSTICE REFORM

Difficult to Believe

Growing up in rural West Tennessee in the Geeter Subdivision near Whitehaven, I was torn about how I wanted to give my life in service to others. I considered becoming a lawyer or a Baptist preacher. I was ambivalent because of competing influences from those close to me. My father, Otis (Aaron) Clayton, worked at the Memphis Navy Yard Cotton-Compress Company. This company processed cotton shipped from the tri-state areas of Tennessee, Arkansas, and Mississippi to make other products, like clothes and furniture. My father worked there as a lead man but was never allowed to be promoted to management because of his race.

Instead, he was required to train younger, entry-level White males to become members of management. His employer discriminated against him by not paying him the amount he deserved. He also became a bootlegger of corn whiskey and a gambler to supplement his salary. He sold corn whiskey from our home in the evenings and on weekends. Invariably, he periodically got into trouble with law enforcement. On one occasion, several Memphis police officers came to our house with a search warrant. Someone had reported that my father was selling corn whiskey in our home. But I had been trained by my father to destroy the whiskey he had stored in the backroom of our home. I took a five-gallon jug of whiskey outside and busted it! However, the police confiscated one pint of whiskey my father forgot in our kitchen. My father was arrested and taken to jail for having illegal corn whiskey with the intent to sell. My mother and PaPa, my fraternal grandfather, later drove downtown to the Memphis city jail and provided bail for my father.

When my father returned home, he addressed me, using my nickname: "Puddin, I will be glad when you grow up because I want you to become a lawyer. I need you to help me fight against these roaches!" (He referred to the police as roaches.) Most evenings, I would sit with my father to watch the CBS Evening News, featuring a famous newsman, Walter Cronkite. My father would point out African-American attorneys like Thurgood Marshall, who exemplified what my father wanted me to become. As an attorney, I could help him and our people to fight the "roaches."

Like you, I grew up in a highly religious community where the center of our lives was the church. My grandfathers on both sides of my family were church deacons. My maternal step-grandmother, Ethel Murphy, was a musician who played for several different local congregations. One of my father's brothers, Columbus (Uncle Bubba), was a preacher. My father's sisters were evangelists and members of their church choir.

As a child and an adolescent, I was always in and out of the church. I attended a tent revival meeting with cousins and relatives one summer evening. We went as guests of my aunt, Willie Mae Clayton-McGowan. She was an evangelist at the Holiness Pentecostal Church. Elder Lusk was her pastor, and he was leading the revival meeting. He customarily led frenzied worship services filled with spirit and music.

It has been many years since that meeting, but I can still hear the words of the song "The Holy Spirit Is in This Place." About midway through the service, Pastor Lusk stood up at the podium. He was a slightly built bald preacher. His spoken words were almost like singing. Pastor Lusk said, "I want all the boys to come down the aisle and stand in front of my podium. I want to pray for all of you. God spoke to me and told me that one of you boys has been called to preach." I have often wondered why he did not ask any young girls to also come down the aisle to the podium. Can God also call girls and women to become preachers? Pastor Lusk continued, "And I want to pray for you all and bless you and rub some oil on your foreheads."

Strange as it may seem, I sensed, at the tender age of ten, that I was the one God had called to become a preacher of the gospel of Christ. But I was terrified and uncertain because I did not believe intuitively that I, as a believer or a preacher, would have to shout, fall to the floor, and round on the floor to prove that I was a follower and minister of

Jesus Christ. Most importantly, because of their lack of preparation for the ministry, I did not know, and I had never met any minister in my Baptist tradition who could provide an intelligent or reasonable understanding of what the call to the ministry is.

It was not until I graduated from LeMoyne Owen College and enlisted in the Air Force that I understood the call to the Christian ministry. I was stationed at the Seymour Johnson Air Force Base in Goldsboro, North Carolina. My father, Edward, had preceded me as a member of the Air Force. He insisted, "When you reach your duty assignment at Seymour Johnson, I recommend you become a member of the base Honor Guard detail. Being a member of this detail will prevent you from being assigned any other base detail. In some base details, enlisted men must ride and walk around the installation picking up cigarette butts and trash.

When I arrived at Seymour Johnson, I volunteered to become a base Honor Guard detail member. This proved to be a blessing in disguise. I met my first African-American chaplain, who was on base detail. He was a Baptist minister who graduated from the Howard University School of Divinity. This minister was a triple threat because he could preach, pray, and sing. In addition, he could play the piano and organ. Indeed, this chaplain was one of the most talented ministers I had ever met.

At that time, we were both swamped performing our other military duties and attending to the needs of our families. Unfortunately, I have forgotten this chaplain's name, but I hope to one day locate him. Like me, he was married and preached weekly at one of the several base chapels. I moved my wife and daughter from Memphis to

Goldsboro. We lived outside the base in a trailer park. This was something to get accustomed to because we had never lived in a trailer home.

I worked during the week on the Seymour Johnson base, and every other weekend, I attended a continuing education master of art graduate program offered on base through Central Michigan University. Although attending graduate school was a burden, the Air Force paid for it. I still had my military educational benefits for forty-eight months when I completed my active duty.

The chaplain I met and became friends with allowed me to ask him questions. I wanted to know him essentially two things—what exactly is a call to the ministry and how I could become a chaplain in the Air Force or any military branch.

"Airman Clayton, this is basically what the call to the Christian ministry is all about: You commit to serving God and the people of God. Also, it means that you must prepare yourself for leadership by studying at the seminary of your choice. And, to become a chaplain in the Air Force or other military branches, you must be an ordained minister, which you can achieve with the help of your pastor and congregation. Then, you must obtain an ecclesiastical endorsement from the National Baptist Convention, USA, Incorporated.

Almost one year before leaving active duty in the United States Air Force at Little Rock Air Force Base in Jacksonville, Arkansas, I made an application to both the Southern University School of Law in Baton Rouge, Louisiana and Vanderbilt University dual master of divinity/juris doctorate program. I was accepted at Southern University, but my application to Vanderbilt University was rejected. I did not attempt to move to Baton Rouge because my wife was totally against it. She was ready to return to Memphis to be among her family and friends.

Studying Theology with a Focus on Homiletics and My Discomfort with an Advisor

When I arrived to pursue doctoral studies at Vanderbilt University School of Divinity, Professor David Buttrick—David as he is called affectionately—was serving as the major professor in the Department of Homiletics. David is an Anglo-American, homiletical preacher in the Presbyterian Church USA and the son of George Buttrick, a great preacher who taught preaching at Union Theological Seminary as a colleague of outstanding scholars like Paul Tillich and Reinhold Niebuhr. These tremendous scholars helped George Buttrick to train his son, David, as he prepared for the ministry.

Consequently, when I became one of his students, David was identified as one of the top teachers of preachers in the world. He had no problem explaining that he enjoyed a certain excitement for the Black preaching tradition. David hesitantly argued, "Otis, I believe that the best preachers in the world are Black preachers. Their experience as fighters for freedom for themselves, their people, and all Americans is expressed eloquently in their delivery. Martin Luther King Jr. is among many in the great preaching pantheon."

However, David rendered me a great disservice when he assigned Assistant Professor Robert Eugene to become my advisor. He was an African American raised in the

Presbyterian Reform Tradition and became an Episcopalian priest. Professor Eugene became a faculty member and taught courses at the divinity school while working to complete his doctoral degree at Princeton University. Nonetheless, David assigned Professor Eugene to become my advisor, and immediately, I became disgruntled with Professor Eugene. He gave me the impression that he saw no value in and had no appreciation for the African-American religious experience. "Otis," he insisted, "you keep trying to mix apples and oranges. You cannot do that in preaching."

"But," I responded, "I am interested in a holistic perspective about preaching because I believe that is what effective preaching is about. It appeals to the congregation's members' minds, bodies, and souls." Unlike David, Professor Eugene used every opportunity to attack and accuse the Black preaching tradition and, more specifically, my perspective on Black preaching. Moreover, when I presented my doctoral thesis proposal to him, "Therapy: The Call and Response Motif in Black Preaching," he rejected it, insisting that there was no such thing as that in preaching."

Given the kinds of confrontations that we were having, I needed to do something quickly; otherwise, with Professor Eugene as my advisor, I would never graduate from Vanderbilt University. I spoke to David. "I need to have a conference with you and Professor Sutton to discuss our various understanding of preaching and Black preaching in particular."

During our meeting, David told Professor Eugene, "Robert, I think you need to discontinue attaching Otis's view of preaching. Otis's position on preaching is just as valid as yours or mine. Please leave Otis alone." Subsequently, after our meeting, David replaced Professor Eugene as my advisor, which allowed me to eventually graduate from Vanderbilt University expeditiously.

Vanderbilt University to Canterbury Christ Church University: Now the Porch Experience

I met Robert Long t initially at the Divinity Library at the Vanderbilt University Divinity School. He worked part-time and served as a writing tutor for students who needed his assistance. Robert is originally from Los Angeles, California. He had completed an engineering degree at the University of California (Davidson) and a master of divinity degree at the University of San Francisco. While I was pursuing my doctoral studies in homiletics, Robert was pursuing a Ph.D. in the Hebrew Bible with a specific focus on New Testament studies. However, I had no detailed understanding that my research papers had to be written and arranged within a particular format. The research papers I submitted to my professors for all classes were returned to me with grades of C+ and B-. I knew my grades at this level would not be tolerated for too long. The dean of the divinity school would eventually expel me from the university because I failed to maintain a grade average of B and above.

I consulted with Larry about the dilemma. "Brother Robert, may I talk with you privately for a moment?" When he agreed, I continued, "I am constantly receiving grades of C+ and B- from my professors. I do not have time to attend the writing laboratory in the evening because of my work schedule, but if my grades do not improve, I will eventually be kicked out of the university. What do you suggest I do?"

"Brother Otis," Robert replied, "I'll tell you what to do. You continue to write your research papers for each class. Then, you give me a copy of what you have written. I will then revise your papers and place each in the appropriate formal style for a small monetary fee. After all, time is money. Money is time."

We agreed with this format and procedure. Shortly after that, my grades improved substantially. They skyrocketed to B+ and sometimes A. When I completed my course, I had also to write and submit a thesis proposal. Larry assisted me with preparing the document and getting it submitted to David and my doctoral thesis committee for approval. It was approved and accepted with flying colors. With Robert's tutorial assistance over four years, I completed and submitted my thesis, "Therapy: The Call and Response Motif in Black Preaching," and graduated with distinction.

Several years later, I was allowed to pursue post-doctoral studies at Canterbury Christ Church University (CCCU) in Canterbury, England. Although I did not consult you before submitting my application, you authored and submitted a letter of recommendation to the university on my behalf. Surprisingly, because of your support and that of other colleagues in academia, I was accepted to study theology at the CCCU.

Of course, this meant I would have to move from Aurora, Colorado, to Canterbury, England. I rented my house and moved into student housing at CCCU. Also, since Larry was one of the persons who wrote a letter of recommendation for me, we had a telephone conversation. He agreed to assist me as a writing tutor for a monetary fee. He would review and revise my research papers before I submitted them to my first reader or advisor at CCCU. Interestingly and sadly, Robert's tutorial monetary fees became more expensive. He even enticed me to sign a contract to continue his assistance.

I said to myself, *Otis, what are you going to do? You have retired from the Department of Veterans Affairs. You are using your veteran education benefits to pay for some of your expenses. You have established a relationship with faculty, staff, and fellow students. You cannot simply drop out of CCCU. You are nearly five thousand miles away from home.* However, although I became melancholy, I decided to exercise my faith in God. I prayed and meditated.

Shortly, therefore, my military injuries began to catch up with me. I had, for nearly twenty years, put off having a necessary spinal surgical procedure. I was taking the medication meloxicam, which eventually caused internal bleeding. I had to be hospitalized for eight days. Upon my release from the hospital, I caught an American Airlines flight back to America to meet with Dr. Juris, my orthopedic surgeon. He stated, "Otis, here are your MRI results. You have a bulging disk at the L-4/L-5 spinal segment. I am going to remove that bad disc and do a spinal fusion that will relieve your pain."

My parents, grandparents, preachers, and other ancestors say, "God takes care of old folks and fools." At that point in my life, I more than likely fell into both those categories— old and foolish. Nevertheless, because of my surgery, I ultimately decided to take a medical leave of absence from CCCU for surgery and rehabilitation. In the process, my medical situation released me from any obligation to my previous writing tutor, Larry George.

In the future, I promised myself and God that, at my first opportunity, I would locate a writing community to help me become a better writer. Consequently, I learned that Vanderbilt University had a Creative Writing Department, and I saw the name of Professor Loraine, who is of Latin-American descent. I also had an interest in learning to speak Spanish. I emailed Professor Lopez and explained that I had graduated from the Vanderbilt University School of Divinity and desired to improve my writing skills. In her email, she noted, "Otis, I do not believe you need to become a student within my department. I believe that The Porch is the best place for you. Susan Felts and Katie McDougall are the founders of that writing community. I know they have classes that will suit your purpose."

Now, I am achieving what I wanted to accomplish at CCCU. I presented a proposal for a thesis that I did not complete. I have subsequently translated that proposed thesis idea into a personal narrative called *Toward a Political Theology: A Multigenerational Memoir.*

Fiftieth Anniversary: Remembering the Historic March across the Edmund Pettis Bridge

I remain excited that you and your loving wife, Jackie, invited me to meet both of you in Selmer, Alabama, for the upcoming fiftieth anniversary of the march across the Edmund Pettis Bridge. It is interesting to note that your marriage has lasted more than four decades. You share a common historical background as you are both from the South, but you met in the great state of New York. You were born and spent your early years in the state of Alabama.

You completed high school and college at a predominately historically Black institution. After graduating from Talladega College with honors, you attended Colgate-Rochester Seminary in Rochester, New York. It is illuminating that you are an alumnus of the same seminary as Martin Luther King Jr. While a student in seminary, you were taught by professors who had also taught him. Next, you became a post-graduate student at Northwestern University, where you earned a Ph.D. in church history.

I recalled it was during your matriculation through Colgate-Rochester Seminary that you met and married your wife, Jackie Law. Admittedly, Jackie, like you, has had an interesting background. She completed her high school education at O'Bannon High School in Greenville, Mississippi, and won a scholarship to study at the prestigious Wilberforce College in Wilberforce, Ohio. No, I am unable to forget my student days at Vanderbilt University. You and Jackie permanently extended your Southern hospitality and generosity to me and my family. You often invited us to your beautiful home for food, fellowship, and interesting intellectual conversations.

We lodged at different locations before meeting for the Selma march across the Edmund Pettis Bridge and other events. Though you could have resided with relatives in the family home of your birth in Camden, Alabama, you and Jackie elected to stay at the Quincy Hotel in Selma. After the march across the bridge, you were scheduled as the keynote speaker for your class reunion. This made perfect sense for you to lodge in Selma. On the other hand, because I am a retired United States Army officer, I secured lodging at the Maxwell-Gunter Air Force Base in Montgomery, Alabama, approximately fifty miles from Selma.

Because of health concerns, none of us—you, Jackie, or I—made the historic walk across the Edmund Pettis Bridge, but we did make it to two other events, the Selma Courthouse and the crowed Tabernacle Baptist Church. We observed Reverend Jessie at both events. Although I have seen him in the newspapers and on television since my teenage years, I have become increasingly suspicious of him for some strange reason. I get the impression that Reverend Jessie enjoys being in the spotlight because he often has nothing meaningful and significant to do or say to resolve prevailing social or political problems.

A Kingian View of the Climate Debate

You are one of the most outstanding Martin Luther King Jr. scholars today. You have written between sixty and a hundred articles and collaborated on over fifteen books about King. Your most recent publication is *The Arc of Truth: The Thinking of Martin Luther King Jr.* You may recall that, as a student at Vanderbilt University, I took a course from you called "Martin Luther King Jr. and the Social Role of Religion."

I ascertained from your class that King was a highly educated African-American preacher in the Black folk tradition who used religion to accomplish things socially and politically. He was the son and grandson of preachers, and he learned and absorbed from them the cultural tradition and practice of the Black preacher. But he also borrowed highly from Anglo-American preaching tradition. In this regard, King was an exemplary model of a preacher who synthesized the best of the African-American and Anglo-American preaching traditions. His speech delivered at the Lincoln Monument in Washington DC called "I Have a Dream" is a classic example of this exciting synthesis.

I vehemently insist that King was more than just a preacher and pastor. After all, he was one of the most influential civil rights movement leaders because of his leadership and service as the president of the Southern Christian Leadership Conference. In the process, he was able to cooperate with other civil rights organizations, labor unions, the United States Congress, and the United States president to obtain the passage of the historic 1964 Civil Rights Bill to secure the right to vote for African Americans. King has been, moreover, an example of phenomenal leadership. As a nation, we celebrate him annually on Martin Luther King Jr. Day.

I greatly appreciate you informing me that King offered some insight into the justice reform debate regarding climate. He believed that humankind must exercise stewardship of the earth. I think that his perspective implies that humanity must work in cooperation with God to resolve the climate issue. God is not a dictator; neither are we God's puppets. Therefore, humankind has the free will to work countlessly toward a solution for climate justice.

I look forward to hearing from you if you have any additional insight related to climate reform.

Printed in the United States
by Baker & Taylor Publisher Services